*The
Making
of a
Modern
Educator*

By William Van Til

TRAVEL	The Danube Flows Through Fascism Foldboat Holidays (contributor)
TEXTBOOKS	Economic Roads for American Democracy Time on Your Hands Modern Education for the Junior High School Years (with others)

YEARBOOKS OF THE ASSOCIATION
FOR SUPERVISION AND CURRICULUM DEVELOPMENT

Americans All (contributor)
Toward a New Curriculum (contributor)
Leadership Through Supervision (contributor)
Forces Affecting American Education
(editor and contributor)

YEARBOOKS OF THE NATIONAL COUNCIL
FOR THE SOCIAL STUDIES

Democratic Human Relations (co-editor
and contributor)
The Study and Teaching of American History
(contributor)
Education for Democratic Citizenship
(contributor)

YEARBOOKS OF THE JOHN DEWEY SOCIETY

Intercultural Attitudes in the Making
(co-editor and contributor)
Educational Freedom in an Age of Anxiety
(contributor)

UNIT	Democracy Demands It (with others)
SPEECH	Great Human Issues of Our Times (contributor)
SELECTIONS	The Making of a Modern Educator

William Van Til

The

Making of a

Modern Educator

THE **BOBBS-MERRILL** COMPANY, INC.
A SUBSIDIARY OF HOWARD W. SAMS & CO., INC.
Publishers • INDIANAPOLIS • NEW YORK

The lines on page 202 are from "The Road Not Taken" from *Complete Poems of Robert Frost*. Copyright 1916 by Henry Holt & Company, Inc. Copyright renewed 1944 by Robert Frost.

"Railroads and Rivers" is reprinted from *The Danube Flows Through Fascism*. Copyright 1938 Charles Scribner's Sons. Used by permission of Charles Scribner's Sons.

ACKNOWLEDGMENTS

"The School Council" originally appeared in *The Clearing House*, XIII (May 1939), 524-526.

"The Shaping of Their Modern Minds" originally appeared as "The Making of Their Modern Minds" in *Social Education*, III (October 1939), 467-472.

"Credo in Action" originally appeared in *The Peabody Journal of Education* (January 1952), 212-228.

"Hostel Travel" originally appeared as "Hostel Vacation" in *Progressive Education*, XXII (April 1945), 16-19; "Youth Hosteling in Ohio," XVIII (February 1941), 99-101; "The Intellectually Gifted Child," XXXIV (July 1957), 124-125.

"Youth Visits Industrial Detroit" originally appeared in *Educational Method* (March 1939).

"The Remarkable Culture of the American Educators" originally appeared in *Educational Leadership* (January 1950), 273-275; "The Ladder of Success in Universities" (May 1951), 497-501; "A Fable of Textbook Strategy" (January 1948), 215-220; "John Dewey's Disciples" (December 1949), 201-202; "The Climate of Fear" (October 1949), 73-75; "The Nashville Story" (May 1958), 481-485; "Let's Communicate Democratic Education" (April 1950), 494-495; "Curriculum Improvement: Who Participates?" (March 1954), 335-337; "Combating Juvenile Delinquency through the Schools" (March 1956), 363-367.

"Educational Freedom in an Age of Anxiety" originally appeared as a Preface to the book of that title, the Twelfth Yearbook of the John Dewey Society (Harper & Brothers, 1953), xiii-xviii. By permission of the publisher.

5

"Attitudes toward Teacher Education" originally appeared as "Critical Attitudes toward Teacher Education" in *History of Educational Journal*, VI (Summer 1955), 244-255.

"Intercultural Attitudes in the Making" originally appeared as Chapter VII in the book of that title, the Ninth Yearbook of the John Dewey Society (Harper & Brothers, 1946), edited by William Heard Kilpatrick and William Van Til, 176-184. By permission of the publisher.

"Toward Democratic Human Relations" was first published in *Great Human Issues of Our Times*, IV, 89-101. Used by permission of George Peabody College for Teachers.

"Interracial Tension in Nashville" by Jon Van Til, originally appeared in *The Swarthmore Phoenix* (April 9, 1960). Reprinted by permission of *The Swarthmore Phoenix*.

"Of Protons, Planes and Presley" is reprinted by permission of the Association for Childhood Education International, 3615 Wisconsin Avenue, N. W., Washington 16, D. C. From *Childhood Education*, XXXIII (May 1957), No. 9, 408-411.

"Better Curriculum—Better Discipline" originally appeared in *National Education Association Journal*, XLV (September 1956), 345.

"The Teaching of American History" originally appeared in Chapter V in *The Study and Teaching of American History*, the Seventeenth Yearbook of the National Council for the Social Studies, 68-72. Reprinted by permission of the National Council for the Social Studies.

"Improving Human Relations in the School Program" originally appeared in *The Instructor*, LXVI (October 1956), 16ff. Used by permission of *The Instructor*.

"Social and Cultural Developments Influence the Curriculum" originally appeared in part in the 1960 *Yearbook* of The American Association of Colleges for Teacher Education, 146-157. Used by permission of the Association.

For Bee and the trio:
Jon, Barbara, Roy

FOREWORD

THE reading of this collection of essays has given me a great deal of pleasure. If I analyze this welcome feeling, I must emphasize three points.

One is that it has been a stimulating experience. The manuscript throughout is refreshing both as to style and as to what it reveals about its author. In style, it is witty in the sense of several of Webster's definitions of the term: it is "possessed of learning"; it is "quick or ready in the perception of amusing points of view and of intelligently entertaining congruities and incongruities"—especially the latter; it is "cleverly novel in expression." What the manuscript mirrors in respect to its author is the image of a man well into middle age who has held fast to the high ideals of his youth.

A second attraction is that the manuscript contains much good red meat. Virtually all the essays within these covers will leave their readers at least a little better—in most cases, much better—equipped to think their way through some important problem of democratic education. There is no pussyfooting; the basic issues are made clear; scholarship is brought to bear on whatever the problem. Especially outstanding in these respects, it seems to me, are the essays in Parts IV, V, and VII of this volume.

My third point is entirely personal—one that the reader cannot share. It is that I had some small part in launching Bill Van Til on his teaching career and in helping him make some of his moves up the vocational ladder, so I feel that some of the credit for the way he has developed belongs to me—an invalid assumption, perhaps, but one that my vanity will not permit me to discard. So I found myself glowing with pride as I made my way through the manuscript—as who wouldn't if he could persuade himself that he had played some casual role? The evidence of dedication to the cause of democratic education, of skill in analysis, of illumination of idea, and of willingness to stand up and be counted is abundant in all the essays which treat of professional matters.

Nor can I expect the reader fully to share my pleasure in reading Part VI of this work—unless perchance he too was in and out of the Van Til household while the ebullient Jon, Barbara, and Roy were sharing the troubled joys of growing up together under the indulgent eye of Bee, the wise and imperturbable mother.

HAROLD C. HAND
University of Illinois

PREFACE

As a teacher of teachers I specialize on learning experiences provided by elementary and secondary schools. The educators have a word for it—the curriculum.

For more than twenty-five years I have been writing for members of my profession. I have had my share in the work of scholarship through writing yearbooks, textbooks, reports of research, reviews of the findings of research.

But I have also written shorter pieces, less formal, usually less solemn, more colloquial and relaxed. Such columns, articles, essays and occasional chapters, gathered in this book, reflect my stubborn belief that one can write simultaneously to teachers and to the general reader. Where did we ever get the idea that education always must be written about in the trade jargon called pedaguese? Throughout the years, I have written to my fellow professionals and, over their shoulders, to the general reader. This book brings together such writing and is directed to a twain which must meet, the profession and the public. May my lapses into jargon be few and be charitably forgiven!

I recognize that collections of shorter writings are in a tradition more familiar to the humanities and the natural and social sciences and less familiar to education. Yet I am not remotely apologetic. Name me an enterprise more vital to mankind than the education of the young.

In a sense, this book is autobiographical, at least of the professional segment of my life. In the aspects of my experience reported here I have invested substantial blood, sweat and tears. I have taken as profit a personal fulfillment, an occasional intimation of contribution to others, and considerable amusement. I anticipate still more such rewards of the teacher.

The Making of a Modern Educator grew out of a conviction of mine. I believe strongly that educators too must be heard by both the profession and the public in the era of the Great Debate

on education. The angry men who write angry books on education should be granted no monopoly; anger is a poor substitute
for personal acquaintance with elementary and secondary schools.
My earnest hope is that my book will make some contribution to
a more relaxed, a better humored and a better informed discussion of education.

WILLIAM VAN TIL
New York University

CONTENTS

I
Teaching in an Experimental School

The Background

IN 1933 I was about to graduate from Columbia College. My major was English, my minor was economics, my hankering was journalism. Naturally, I intended to write The Great American Novel.

During that senior undergraduate year I decided to take out some unemployment insurance. So I "crossed the street" for a few education courses. The street is 120th, the widest street in the world, according to Columbia legend, because it separates the rest of Columbia University from Teachers College.

My classmates scoffed and my liberal arts professors frowned. A Mark Van Doren advisee, of all people, "crossing the street"! The imminent corruption of my academic purity was foretold.

I enjoyed my corruption and I worshipped my corrupters. Directing my student teaching were Verna Carley, an educational and social liberal and an educator who treated each student as an individual person, and Harold Hand, a young man with fire in his whiskers, who was later to become "the flying professor" of the University of Illinois and to pilot himself in his single-motor plane the equivalent of several times round the world for consultative and speaking engagements in American school systems.

Proud possessor of my B.A. in liberal arts and minimally certified for teaching, I discovered on graduation from Columbia College that I was part of the statistics I had studied in economics. I was unemployed. My applications for jobs in journalism grew mountainous.

I fell back on my version of unemployment insurance and in November of 1933 the State of New York decided to pay me seventy-five dollars a month and keep as a teacher. Where? In a reform school for delinquent boys, the bitter hostile products of the New York City slums.

In retrospect, I wouldn't swap the experience I had for any other beginning. Now, that is—not then. I learned to teach the hard way. My scholarship in Will Shakespeare and Thorstein

17

Veblen was not exactly relevant to teaching delinquents. I learned what every effective teacher must learn and what few of education's self-appointed critics have learned—you start with youngsters where they are if you are to help them climb.

I survived. Sometimes I even think I helped. After a year I was better prepared for my first sustained teaching experience in a quite different school, the shining new school established on the campus of Ohio State University as a laboratory for experimentation with new practices in elementary and secondary school teaching. If you want to call it a progressive school I won't object, provided the modifier doesn't bias you in advance.

For nine years at Ohio State University School, 1934-1943, I taught social studies, English, and a problem-centered course called "core" which cut across several subjects. I really learned about teaching during those years of freedom to teach junior high school and senior high school students.

Yet all too often a teacher's best experiences go unrecorded. Absorbed in the excitement of kindled minds and swept up in the flow of daily responsibilities, we teachers keep no journals. With time, recollection blurs and the experiences are lost to all—except, we hope, those whom the experiences helped to shape.

So, all too few are my accounts of freedom to experiment in teaching in the laboratory school. Several that I published as a young educator are gathered here with no attempt to "update" them, a clumsy word for a phony practice popular with essayists and editors. After all, they are not intended to be used as lesson plans by a literal-minded teacher in tomorrow's class. If, through these accounts, the reader can sense some of the excitement of a free teacher working with free learners, they will have served for greater understanding of what modern education means.

⋖§ One of the paradoxes of the profession is that some of the better learning experiences for students are often developed in extra-curricular activities—that wing added to the educational structure to house the realistic and vital interests of youth which are deemed by genteel educators to be too vigorous or too vulgar to come into the main house. Such were the learning experiences of the School Council of Ohio State University School after Director Rudolph D. Lindquist informed the members that Santa Claus was dead.

1 *The School Council*

THE newly formed school council—twelve student members and two faculty members—came out of a fall night to a meeting in the Ohio State University School.

We knew little of what our work would be. As a faculty member, I had an inadequate idea that high-school councils were to represent student opinion and to disburse money from some vague fund for student activities.

At the first meeting we seemed to have little on the agenda; the council promised to be a tedious, useless expenditure of time—so after someone casually mentioned finances and we delegated a committee to check with the administration on moneys to disburse for student activities, we adjourned early.

The finance committee wore a troubled expression at our next meeting. They reported that the new council representing the school was several hundred dollars in debt, for the former council had invested money in activities such as dances and plays which were socially and artistically, but not financially, successful. And when the committee had approached the director with a request for money from student fees that newspapers, magazines, plays, operettas, dances, Christmas festivals, and assemblies might continue, the members had been informed quite understandably by the director that Santa Claus was dead and that no fund would be forthcoming.

Though the council did not realize it at that time, those clipped words created the opportunity for a meaningful school council. Running school activities with money from mysterious administrative sources was over. Balancing a budget, taxing, banking, lending on interest, collecting, spending, policy-making in regard to profits became realistic council functions.

The council directly taxed the students for the year's expenses, and the council and the school learned that a governmental body without coercive power can collect from the 95 per cent who are good citizens but cannot collect from the dissident 5 per cent. We added this item to our growing store of knowledge about government.

The council sponsored a play to pay off the debt and I had a glimpse of functional education. Council members served on hard-working committees in charge of dramatic arrangements and made certain that committee deliberations and decisions represented their best thinking. For the group endeavor was actual and the penalty for failure not theoretical but hard and tangible.

I remember the group when a fleeting carelessness lost the enterprise ten dollars. The money as money did not matter; we stood to gain nothing material by success. The money as a symbol of the larger enterprise did matter. It was a quantitative standard of the success of a venture to aid a whole school. Our interest in dollars was akin to a statesman's interest in building the maximum number of roads and school houses with the minimum amount of public money.

The school council now had a vital social purpose, and here the council seemed to hold an advantage over the field of education in which I usually trafficked. With all our efforts in schools we seldom can achieve better than a semi-artificial situation where failure in responsibility does not penalize as it does in life.

After the play succeeded and the debt vanished, a new problem arose. The council had experimented with an admission charge to basketball games as a fund-raising device. No less a group than the school faculty questioned the council's authority to inaugurate this policy. Armed with the council constitution, council members took part in a faculty meeting.

At first it seemed that the issue was whether the council was governing or playing at governing. But with deeper inquiry, the issue was shown to be a matter of correct procedure in the event that a council decision, though sanctioned by the constitution of the school body, conflicted with a policy that had originated with faculty and administration.

The council thought that a charge for basketball games would be a way of promoting school spirit and promoting the general welfare of the school, in accordance with the council constitution. To the faculty, school games were part of the athletic program and thereby of the curriculum, and a charge would tinge games with the commercialism and overemphasis on competitive athletics that the faculty wished to avoid.

The problem was discussed at length and, content that the students wished equally to avoid commercialism and that the purposes of the charge and the destination of the fund were commendable, the faculty modified the policy. A general principle which came out of the discussion was that any other difference which might arise would be adjusted by a joint meeting.

Since those days, I have read in important journals many sage essays, always of course by teachers, on the degree of democracy to be allowed a school council. The essays usually disagree only on the point at which the adult authors would exercise the sovereign authority they assume is rightfully theirs. To paraphrase Oscar Wilde, some contributors laud democracy in theory and ape dictatorship in practice—and that's so important in education nowadays.

Most of the essays might be summed up in "We believe in democracy, but . . ." Their authors forget that democracy in a school should be the joint concern of student and faculty; neither anarchy nor autocracy need characterize student-council relationships to faculty and administration.

A body with student and faculty members, which stays within legal bounds set forth by its constitution and does not conflict with accepted school policy, should, like any other parliamentary body, make decisions and accept responsibility for its actions.

Overstepping constitutional bounds or clashing with accepted policy should be handled reasonably by the joint-meeting technique or by a veto legally provided for in the constitution of the school body. It is not merely that the council should be "allowed" this status by a principal and faculty—a council has a democratic right to such a position in a democratic school system. How else than through practice can self-government and responsibility for a democratic society be fostered?

Toward the end of the year, meetings between the council and the faculty, and between the council and entire student body were no longer rarities. An old and vexing University School problem was settled: whether, in a school that stressed intramural sports, athletic letters should be given to athletes who represented University School in competitive athletics. After deliberation through open meetings, a plan was drafted which provided for awards for distinguished activity in many fields, including scholarship.

The school body was asked who was to pay for the first batch of awards, athletic letters. The students replied, "The council through our tax money." No one voted for Santa Claus. For Santa Claus was dead.

These things stand out: I have never seen cooperation, responsibility, social thinking, initiative, problem solving, and courage so develop and flourish as under the tyranny of our economy regime; never did I teach so much relevant and meaningful social science (even in the subject-matter sense) as when we made analogies between our constitution and the federal Constitution, between our proposed supreme court and federal Supreme Court, between our debt and governmental debts, and scores of other analogies to help our thinking. There is probably a moral somewhere.

❧ The study of how we arrive at our ideas is perennially fascinating to high school youth. It combines social understanding with insight into that most important person in every individual's life—himself. For English and social studies teachers, the study of public opinion is a "natural." The Shaping of Their Modern Minds is based on junior and senior social studies classes at Ohio State University School.

2 *The Shaping of Their Modern Minds*

MANY men and many institutions have contributed to the shaping of a modern's mind. If he is to use that mind fruitfully, he has to understand its making and why he believes what he does. To be educated, he must clear his mind of underbrush, understand his sources of education and of miseducation, and evaluate them and their progeny—his beliefs and attitudes.

A class I taught demonstrated nicely the need for this, and equally the fact that this is a very difficult thing to do. We were attempting to survey, in a twelfth grade, the range of solutions to American social-economic dilemmas proposed by thinkers from Right to Left, and we aimed to stimulate each student to build toward a philosophy satisfactory for both himself and society. Theoretically, each was to ponder goals; each was to seek methods complementary to goals and adapted to the facts of modern American life.

Yet mental blocks kept arising between the student mind and the printed page. Personal considerations appeared, unacknowledged, in student thinking—personal considerations like the size of father's small or considerable income and the grip of the family on the slippery ladder of polite society. In the battle of ideas, things once heard, and thereafter firmly held, manned the ramparts beside—and against—demonstrable truths. Hobgoblin phrases from the editorial columns did a dance macabre in discussion. Attitudes derived from the lively arts elbowed in, the sugared persuasions of the darkened movie theatres as to the nature of the good life, the blare of the orators who played with old, old words the old, old tunes that had lost their meaning but not their existence when the frontier closed. Therefore many students found it difficult to fulfill the group purpose, to mold facts, beliefs, and attitudes into unified and reasonable philosophies.

The sad truth was that there were few, if any, uncommitted minds present. This was the twentieth century, and these youngsters were seventeen. Already they had philosophies, well knit or loose, articulate or dumb, but, nevertheless, philosophies. And they clung to them. To a large extent, their minds had been already made up, during their unsuspicious years, by a mélange of education and miseducation, passion and clarified thought, prejudice and blunt fact. They had heard, as had their ancestors over the centuries, the songs of an ancient trinity of institutions: the family, the church, the school. These youngsters had also been inculcated with a morality that was to serve as armor and shield in the struggle among life's contradictions. New voices, however, had been added to the chorus, and the old voices sounded differently. The tones of family and church were ringing less resoundingly in their ears, and educators in the decade could begin an article, as one had recently, by declaring that "the school is a relatively unimportant cultural institution." To some sociologists it seemed that the trinity of family, church, and school was disintegrating; to others, the old voices seemed muted by lusty new choristers—the products of a twentieth-century revolution in communication that was yet in its infancy. In either case, these youngsters had always counted the radio, the movie, the popular magazine, the mass-production newspaper, the book flood, as part of the swelling chorus. They had felt the impact of "propaganda," which was defined by the Institute for Propaganda Analysis as "expression of opinion or action by individuals or groups deliberately designed to influence opinions or actions of other individuals or groups with reference to predetermined ends." And they showed the results.

With recognition, then, of the nature of the primary problem, that opinions already were formed, the group of youngsters in my class attempted to understand why they believed what they did. The results, in terms of a more skeptical and freer spirit, a greater tolerance that came with an appreciation of why people ranged from Right to Left, more critical thought and curious seeking, less defensiveness and sloganizing, were promising. In the following years, other classes experimented with a study of the making of their modern minds. Some techniques found useful in two eleventh grade classes are sketched below as suggestive rather than definitive.

There was a year when a class, after having adopted the study, thought best to begin with group discussion rather than with individual research. Each opinion-forming agency was scrutinized in turn: family, church, school, radio, movie, newspaper, book, magazine, and associates. Every discussion began with the question, "What effect has this agency had on you?" Frankness is considered a virtue in the young, although an indiscretion in the old, so anecdotes aplenty were forthcoming from these unrepressed eleventh graders. A student of adolescent psychology would have chuckled, with his theories confirmed, if he had heard one rebel who spoke up, after much testimony as to sources of beliefs. "All of you have been mentioning how you got your ideas on politics and labor unions from your parents. I must be different, because whenever my mother or father say anything, I automatically believe the opposite."

Early in discussion, someone asked, "But why do we accept or reject other people's ideas so easily? Why don't the suggestions just bounce off us?" So we brought into discussion a skilled English teacher, Dr. Lou LaBrant, who also had a background in psychology. With her, the students worked out a psychology course in miniature and grew familiar with such basic concepts as conditioning, rationalization, and the influence of heredity and environment on man. The study of agencies and of social psychology continued on alternate days.

After a group has surveyed the agencies of public opinion, and after it has surveyed man's susceptibility, it is ready to deal with techniques by which these agencies mold the mind. A primary technique is the stereotype, "the picture in your head" that attributes "group characteristics" to each separate member of a group. Walter Lippmann made a contribution to thought on the formation of public opinion when he described stereotyping in his *Public Opinion* and *The Phantom Public*.

To introduce the stereotype, an old psychological trick was used with similar results in both classes. A disorderly scene—carefully planned in advance—was quickly introduced, enacted, and ended. One bizarrely dressed student quite unexpectedly chased another through the classroom. The startled students were asked to describe just what had occurred. Of course, they added details and they omitted details. Many saw the boys normally dressed as they knew them in everyday school life. There were as many versions of the shouted words that accompanied the act as there were students in the room—and all wrong. We thought over the fact that the time span of the incident was that of a typical accident.

We speculated on the fact that a man has difficulty describing with any high degree of accuracy an incident that takes place before his own eyes, yet he firmly holds beliefs on any number of immensely complicated abstractions about things that he has never seen, heard, felt, or smelled. What human being cannot describe for us a "fascist," or a "communist," or a "school teacher," or the character of "Negroes," "Jews," or "Irishmen"? Who cannot tell us whether these abstractions are "good" or "bad": "inflation," "government spending," "labor unionism" and a host of others?

So we discussed stereotypes at length, how a word or an action creates a certain "picture in our heads," and how we react to the picture as though it were reality, how we identify a person or idea with a handy, over-simplified generalization and react to the short-cut abstraction rather than to separate individual entities. Lists of stereotypes were compiled and a few were analyzed critically, including the "anarchist." This character proved to be a dirty fellow, with black whiskers, black felt hat, smoking bomb, a soapbox, and, on his sneering lips, a shout, "Down with everything!"

Classes talked of the limited validity of stereotypes. They examined the exceptions to the stereotype, such as the *honest* "politician," the *generous* "Jew" (or "Scotchman"), the *likeable* "fascist," and noted how the person who has stereotyped is confused till he puts the difficulty down with the sage observation, "the exception proves the rule." They discussed the manner in which people dismiss those who, amazingly, refuse to share with them their firmly held stereotypes, as "he is losing his mind," "he is afraid for his job," "he sold out to the owning class," "he is a nigger lover."

A kindred technique frequently used by those who would consciously or unconsciously mold the minds of men is the liberal use of emotional words. Like stereotypes, emotional words are commonly accepted substitutes for thought. They call up positive or negative reactions in the listener and are intended to have a maximum of emotional punch and a minimum of intellectual meaning. Tie a negative emotional word or stereotype to the coat tails of an opponent or to a law or an idea, succeed in having the citizen associate the negative expression with the opponent or law or idea, and the propagandist's game is practically won.

Editorial columns and sometimes even news columns furnish handy case studies. Students have asked themselves, "Does the speech, editorial, article, news story make you feel negative or positive toward the subject under consideration? Exactly how has this been done? What reasoning do you accept and what do you reject?"

Some student groups, after introductory lectures and discussions, have read widely. Classes have, at times, gone superficially or more deeply into individual student research, have undertaken such studies as "propaganda in education," "the consumer," an analysis of the policies of the two leading newspapers in Columbus towards social and political questions, or "how the newspapers influence public opinion."

Some teachers who see the importance of training students to cope with propaganda in modern society disagree as to the proper technique, whether to stress critical thought throughout the curriculum or to concentrate on courses in propaganda analysis. To my mind, such a dualism is false, since critical thinking throughout the curriculum is complementary to, not antithetical to, specialized training in the techniques of public opinion. One may provide training in critical thought in a course in mathematics, or in scientific experimentation, or as the central meaning of a play or novel is discussed in an English class. Yet the techniques of public opinion should also be especially emphasized in social science courses. Human psychology may be considered in science classes. Graphs as a means of dramatizing facts and creating an effect may be discussed in mathematics classes as early as junior high school. A ninth-grade language course may discuss the structure of language and the use and meaning of words. People in all teaching fields are welcome to participate in the good fight to help students understand the shaping of their modern minds.

There is a world of work still to be done on this topic in all schools. For instance, it seems to me that students must become acquainted through firsthand information with the workings of pressure groups in the nation and in their community. They must move beyond mere comprehension of the formation of public opinion in a democratic society to an active identification of themselves with forces working for goals which they hold to be good.

Students may take a step forward by hearing representatives present the programs of such bodies as consumers' cooperatives, political parties, church groups, peace groups, labor unions, YMCA's, student federations, Hi-Y's, Girl Reserves, civil liberties groups, organizations dealing with race prejudice, parent-teacher organizations, literary and art clubs, community fund groups and welfare groups. Students will take a stride forward when, after they have examined critically the making of their minds, and—a point to be heavily emphasized—after they have developed a tentative philosophy of requisite maturity which requires testing in the laboratory of life, they are encouraged and aided by the school to identify themselves with suitable groups willing to cooperate which represent the individual's maturing beliefs. With such a broad conception of education, the schools should play a significant role in training the young for intelligent participation in American society.

Let us not forget that the study of public opinion is only one phase, albeit an important one, of education. For those brought up in the American way of life, the quintessence of education, the end to which all phases must contribute, is the continual development and reinterpretation of the democratic philosophy. Only in the light of democratic standards and values arrived at through the free play of intelligence, can the individual use well, in his own life and actions, the knowledge gained through a study of public opinion.

≈§ After twenty-seven years as a professional educator, these things I do believe:

That the over-all purpose of American education is to develop the understanding and practice of democracy as a way of life.

That the salient characteristic of democracy as a way of life is faith in the method of intelligence.

That the best learning experiences are those which begin with the needs of the learner, illuminate the social realities of his time, and contrast competing ways of living.

That teacher-pupil planning is desirable and feasible.

That controversial issues are the life-blood of general education learning experiences.

That indoctrination of set answers to controversial issues, such as indoctrination for laissez faire or for socialism, indoctrination for isolation or for world government, is an abuse of the method of intelligence and thus undemocratic.

That by thinking through, using facts, and applying values, students can reach conclusions for themselves; they need not and must not be innocuous neutrals on human issues.

That, if mature men and women are to act, young men and women must learn to act.

How can one best convey a credo? Faith in high-order abstractions often betrays us when we would communicate. Therefore, this case study illustrating the credo is ventured. Sometimes specifics can make theory real.

So there follows a report of the last high school class this writer taught at the Ohio State University School. Many imperfections were obvious to him years later as he wrote the account from his files of student papers. Yet the class experience is an attempt at the credo in action.

3   *Credo in Action*

As THEY planned their core curriculum experiences, it was obvious that here was a crop of high school seniors who knew what they wanted. Perhaps a study of psychology should be a part of the nine hours weekly of class meetings? No, they decided. Vocations, then? No. Public opinion and propaganda? No. Perhaps a study of fascism, communism, and capitalism (a best seller with senior classes of the late nineteen thirties)? As a proposal for the senior class of 1942-1943, it left them cold. Perhaps sex, morality, and personal relationships? Definitely no, said the seniors.

What then did they choose for study during core periods before most of them went to fight their war in this world they never made? The war background. Military service, war industry, and civilian defense. The home front during the war. Economic and international proposals for the postwar period.

This is a report on one phase of their experiencing—ten weeks of investigation of American economic life and proposed international organization after the war.

It is sensible to begin one's thinking by defining terms and problems, as philosophers like to point out. So on opening their quarter of study on postwar problems, the twenty-nine class members called in a professor of economics, a professor of political science, and Elmer Davis for help. The former two, Drs. Robert Patton and E. Allen Helms, were local university men and generously came to us for discussions. Since Elmer Davis was obviously being harried by Congress and his Office of War Information responsibilities four hundred miles from us, the group imported his voice to the classroom via the recording, "Then Came War: 1939." In work periods the students selected and read pamphlets appropriate to their informational background and academic ability. Representative of the more suitable materials were Public Affairs Pamphlets, Foreign Policy Headline Books and pamphlets of the Commission to Study the Organization of the Peace.

Based upon such sources, as well as the individual's own ideas, a list of postwar problems which he thought important was compiled by each student. A student committee took each list and blended them into a mimeographed master list of ninety-one problems, which accredited in parentheses the student, speaker, or writer who suggested the particular problem. Typical problems, exactly as phrased by various class members, were:

To determine whether a planned economy or a laissez faire system can maintain a balance at the point of full employment.

To help returning soldiers get readjusted and located in the colleges and higher schools of education which they left.

To shoulder the main part of the burden of feeding Europe besides feeding our own country.

To abolish racial discrimination against Negroes and other minorities in the United States.

To control population movements to already overcrowded areas to prevent poverty.

To make aggressive policies too dangerous to be pursued.

To place forces of occupation in the freed nations of Europe after the war and to put a stop to the inevitable epidemic of uprisings.

To form a union of all countries and nations after the war which would eventually accomplish a sound, world-wide, collective security.

To overcome the nationalism that has developed during the war.

To determine the status of countries now under imperialistic rule as a result of the nineteenth century.

To re-educate the people of totalitarian nations to a democratic point of view.

Thinking about social problems without having recourse to values or goals is as impossible as is lifting one's self by the proverbial boot straps—notwithstanding the pious tributes to "complete neutrality" paid by those quixotic members of the education fraternity who prize respectability above common sense. Consequently, having stated their problems, these young people in a democratic society engaged in a war for survival asked themselves, "What am I fighting for and what am I fighting against?" They read statements on war aims typified by expressions from Lin Yutang, Jan Masaryk, Sumner Welles, the Archbishop of Canterbury, the Office of War Information. All heard recorded talks by Clark Eichelberger and Elmer Rice and listened through three dramatized recordings distributed free of charge by the Educational Radio Service of the U. S. Office of Education, including Norman Corwin's widely heard Bill of Rights program, "We Hold These Truths."

Still, when they wrote essays and plays and statements and drew sketches on what they stood for and against, they also wrote and drew from their hearts, not exclusively from authorities. Alex, an Austrian refugee, wrote,

I am fighting against these persons: Karl Pecina, an Austrian illegal Nazi, my teacher; . . . Paul Popp, fifth columnist, my classmate; . . . Hermann Schmidt, my German teacher, Hitler youth leader, sadist; Otto Kellerman, before the Anschluss a fifth rate dealer in furs, afterwards Vienna's first Uniform agent . . .

I am fighting against intolerance, the law that might is right, isolationism, prejudice, cruelty and indifference, war . . .

Kimball, another student, had a character in a radio script say,

I ain't one of these guys that goes around shouting two-bit words about—what is it? Heritage, equality? I know that old man Hitler is out to make things tough for us. But see, I'm one of these guys that likes his three squares a day. I like to go to the show on Thursdays off, with Pearl, me wife, and I like to send me kids to a Catholic school if I want. No, a guy can't measure freedom in phrases and words. He's got to be there to find out those things and us, the little guys, we like this freedom, see? Sure we've had some tough breaks in the last few years, but we like it here and by Mulligan's beard we'll fight like Billy Conn to save it . . .

Phil wrote,

1. Nationalistic as this may sound, my first purpose in fighting is simply to keep the Japs, Germans, and Italians from invading our country. Any other and more humanitarian motives must come second to this.

2. For a more equitable distribution of the world's wealth. The spectacle of 300,000,000 inhabitants of India living at a starvation level while a chosen few in countries with great natural resources live in what is (comparatively) luxury, is, to say the least, not very hopeful. Under this would also come domestic problems of a similar nature. To sacrifice thousands of lives, perhaps millions, and billions of dollars to preserve conditions such as shown in the movie we saw, *The City*, is absurd. This would mean actual economic security . . .

To epitomize what he was against, Griffith introduced a series of voices in radio play scenes.

School teacher: What is the duty of all good Germans?
Pupil: The duty of all Germans is to obey the Führer in what he asks; never to question at any time his commands, and to be ready to die for Hitler if he asks it.
School teacher: Who betrayed us in the last war?
Pupil: The Jews betrayed us in the last war and therefore they are to be extinguished . . .

* * * * *

A Governor: So I say that the Negro is little better than an animal, a badly diseased animal who must be kept from us pure whites, and must be kept in his proper place, that of subservience to the pure white race. So I pledge myself always to fight against any interference with these rights which are only the fit inheritance of the white race.

* * * * *

Member of House of Commons: Do the four freedoms apply to India, sir?
Prime Minister: No, sir.

As Barbara saw it,

I want the right to believe and to act upon whatever belief I hold. In my case the belief is in Christianity and God. I must be able to attend church, to worship and to work to make the Christian principles part of my living.

I want economic freedom or security—not only for myself but for all people. If all people do not have this then I lose part of my security and contentment.

The things I am fighting against are those forces which deprive people of the right, most of all, to think. Those leaders who try to dominate the minds and spirits of men as well as their actions and standards of living are the most dangerous things in the world.

Goals and values are basic. But unless they are implemented by technical understanding and accomplishment, they may be useless verbiage. So each class member read, and listened to fel-

34

low students and the teacher as we looked at possible roads in the future which might be taken by the American economy. To chart the possible courses, students arched semicircles on large sheets of drawing paper. Individually they recorded what they found as to the course that lay farthest left in their diagram, socialism; the course that lay farthest right, completely unregulated laissez faire; and the two middle courses which many economists believed were destined to struggle for dominance in the immediate postwar period. These two approaches were (1) planning by government for a full employment program through governmental and private sponsorship of employment opportunities (typified by the National Resources Planning Board) and (2) leadership by business for jobs and profits through revivified lightly-regulated private enterprise (typified by the Committee for Economic Development).

The right and the left found themselves in disagreement when each student tried to describe the domestic economic system which seemed best as implementation of the individual's values. The following are excerpts representing generalized points of view. Henry, well to the right, saw it this way after study:

I am a believer in very little government control of business. I am strongly in favor of what Fulton Lewis, Jr., calls "the fifth freedom," that is, the freedom of private enterprise. And it is one of the definite things I am fighting for in this war. To me it means that I, or any one else in this country, can go out and start a business by myself and be able to run it the way I see fit and go as far as I wish... If the government begins controlling business, then it seems to me we would be destroying one of the main things that has made America the most wonderful and democratic country in the world, and certainly the thing that has made us the great industrial nation that we are, and that is the capitalistic system.

Tee, a moderate conservative, wrote,

Before I look at the kind of domestic economy I want, let's see what it is I want any system to do, or what my purpose is for the system. Every man should have a certain amount of security and I am looking towards organized business to do it . . .

I want business to organize itself so that whatever it decided will be its decision and not the government's. As I see it, it comes down to the fact that we have either the government handing down the rules and methods of operating a business or a group of individuals make their plans in the framework set down by the government. The federal government will set the wages, hours, and working conditions and it will be up to the businessmen to meet the requirements . . .

You may ask why with the other three types of a society I took what I did. The extreme conservative with "the survival of the fittest" as a motto does not take into account the fact that there must be some planning because too many people will not be "the fittest." Because I want the most amount of people to have a certain amount of security, I am forced to throw out this point of view. Planning for welfare puts the planning into the government's hands. I think the businessmen can take the faults they have made and come out with a constructive way of running a society . . .

Audrey, a middle-of-the-roader, advocated,

Let private enterprise sink its teeth into the ranks of the unemployed first, building airplanes, plastics, Bendix washers, and television, bringing in all the new-fangled gadgets.* I think there will be enough new items on the market along with the old to employ the majority of men coming back from the war. . . The unemployed that are left over can be employed by the government.

I think perhaps business should work out for itself, with the government giving a helping hand to see that private enterprise isn't working for private enterprise, but rather it works for the people. The government should guide and help business as much as possible so that we can attain the goals we are striving to meet. The government can "prime the pump," so to speak, and help in any

* Audrey's incongruous figure of speech reminds me to point out that throughout this book quotations are reproduced exactly as written by individual students, not as later corrected by their teacher. (Did I remember to correct Audrey? I hope so.) Thus the reader may judge for himself students' ideas and communication skills.

way it can. It should also step in any time if it sees fit to do so. For instance, in 1929 . . .

Phil, persuaded of the validity of the planning viewpoint, wrote,

It seems to me that the logical choice is that of planning for welfare. This comes closest to satisfying my goals for the results which an economic system should produce, these being: first, economic security for all, that is, certain minimum of nutrition, health, and living standards below which no human should be allowed to sink. Secondly, an opportunity for advancement and freedom for an individual to rise as high in society as his abilities and ambition will permit him. The laissez faire viewpoint while allowing for (or really emphasizing) the latter goal, has the obvious disadvantage of making possible exploitation of those who haven't sufficient ability to better themselves. Socialism stresses the first goal, but I don't think it sufficiently allows for the individual enterprise drive which, good or bad, does exist. Organized business might be a slightly better solution, but after the fiasco of the thirties I don't believe they can.

Pete adopted the same general pattern as a temporary expedient, but expressed himself vehemently. In his closing sentence he jabbed against the instructor's recurrent advice, "More light and less heat. Let's be analytical about this."

Their (certain industrialists) chief argument is that a slight deviation from the grand old American way of self-manufacture and waiting and hoping, no matter what the benefits accrued by the people, leads straight to fascism and the black pits of a Hitlerian devil! That by instituting a modicum of official control the government is ruthlessly stamping out the priceless American birthright of initiative and private enterprise, regardless of the circumstances under which the regulation is administered! This is not a thing to be faced calmly. This is the greatest subversive element in this country today. These are the men who destroy us —and who would destroy learning and culture in America because of the realization that these are the elements which must some day destroy them. . . . They must be fought with everything we have. And if emotion is an effective weapon it must be used.

37

Now I am sick and tired of the "analytical approach" and say we have done with it!

Off to the left, Mary wrote,

Government ownership does not mean that a man's initiative is destroyed; on the contrary a man would possess more knowing that there is no private man to stop him and like any other man he can obtain a good job, and his children can obtain a good education. The people would be working for the state, but who receives the houses, clothes, food, education and jobs if not the people? In other words we would be working for ourselves.

The senior class of 1943 became as absorbed in competing forms of international organization as senior classes of the fermenting thirties had been absorbed in competing forms of economic systems for America. After an overview conducted through teacher-led discussion which centered on a semicircular chart of possible courses of action developed on the blackboard, the class divided into groups to study isolation, the "good-will policy," Union Now, a revised League of Nations, the United Nations, and world organization. Each student chose the group nearest to his present convictions, met to read and to talk together, then reported with his group. The largest groups were, respectively, world organization, United Nations, and isolation.

The report of the isolationist group was characteristic of the group procedure in the panels which began with isolation and concluded with world organization. The chairman was a lad who had stirred a tornado of protest during our discussion of domestic economies when he had icily inquired, "Why should I give up my steaks to feed some Chinks?" His group mobilized their arguments skillfully, though some students admittedly strayed from the fold of the converted as they read on. They argued: 1) we produce and sell American; only a fraction goes abroad in peacetime, 2) our foreign trade isn't worth a third war, 3) there is plenty of social reconstruction to take care of among our American underprivileged without looking abroad, 4) war is expensive and, with armaments, avoidable for us, 5) the oceans are still good, 6) the United States could achieve self-sufficiency particularly with our present growth of technology in wartime, 7) Europe's quarrels and minority problems are incurable, 8) our historic policy of no entangling alliances, 9) we want to maintain national sovereignty.

The audience seethed restlessly but held its peace. After his summary, the chairman announced, "Open season." Through a barrage of questions the audience inquired whether the panel had heard of 1) the airplane, 2) interdependence, 3) the costliness of a third war as contrasted with the cost of international peace machinery, 4) war aims, 5) decent idealism, 6) democracy and Christianity, 7) the two-time failure of isolation, 8) the superficiality of the traditional policy argument, 9) our need for British naval cooperation. It was a high school version of the historic pre-Pearl Harbor debates in Congress. It was a forecast of the shape of things to come when America resumed the debate at mid-century and Truman, Taft, Acheson, MacArthur and others spoke their convictions.

So the sessions went, in a two weeks which were marked by vigor and by honest efforts to think through possible courses for international relations and foreign policy. Advocates of the "good-will policy" quoted liberally from Herbert Hoover and Hugh Gibson's book, *Problems of a Lasting Peace*, and tried to respond to questions on whether the approach dealt deeply enough with fundamental economic causes of war. Followers of Clarence Streit who read his *Union Now* books and the *Fortune* supplement, "Relations with Britain," had to meet questions on Anglo-Saxon imperialism and on what Orientals and Russians might think of such a combination as Streit advocated. Exponents of a new League of Nations, who used pamphlets of the Commission to Study the Organization of the Peace, were asked to show concretely how the proposed new league would have more vigor and command greater cooperation than the old. Those who saw promise in the continuation of the United Nations into peacetime confined their discussion too largely to past accomplishments and present military needs. As in society at large at that particular moment in history, advocates of United Nations collaboration were unclear as to whether they were advocating an alliance, a league, or the nucleus of a world organization. Representing a comprehensive internationalism were those who called for a World State. Vexed by accusations of "fuzzy idealism" and encouraged by Eli Culbertson's specificity in his *Readers' Digest* article and later pamphlet, several enthusiastic internationalists drew up blueprints for the World State which even tried to determine the number of representatives from each nation, unit, or region.

It is all too easy to look down one's long scholarly nose upon these young people in their jousts with ideas. It is true that the atmosphere was not as learned as that in which the good doctors of political science convene. It is easy to say that topics with which they grappled were too difficult for them. Yet the stubborn, scary fact remains that, in a democracy, decisions on such issues must be made by the common man, not by the good doctors alone. Difficult or not, problems must be faced and studied and the ordinary person must render his judgments. He would be much better equipped if he had even the brief opportunity that these students had to carry his share of the burden of social thinking which is a prerequisite to making a world which, as Henry Adams said, "sensitive and timid natures could regard without a shudder."

Brief excerpts may convey a few of the students' ideas after the series of discussions. Kalman wrote,

In order to plant the seed of democracy in the fascistic countries, we must allow them to have some sort of say-so in what is to be done with them after the war. In this way we can introduce them to democracy through practice instead of force . . .

Stella, a Hawaiian girl of Chinese ancestry, wrote,

Somehow I can't visualize Russia and China, or any other country for that matter, on the sidelines watching the United States and Britain dictate what others should do and thereby running the whole circus. The one point which is brought out in that system—educate the world to our way—doesn't seem to conform to ideas expressed in the Atlantic Charter, that people have the right to choose the form of government they wish to live under.

Marjorie said,

My idea of the most workable international organization would be, in nature, a league. I think it is too soon to think of asking all nations to completely abandon nationalistic tendencies by forming a world state. I not only think this is premature, but I also think it is not completely advisable. The world is so large that a system of total government would be so difficult to manage in all its details that it would have to be subdivided into regions in which self-government could be established . . .

Barbara wrote,

To the people . . . who say that we cannot just suddenly form an organization of the whole world I would point out that if 13 colonies could do it in 1776, then there is at least a basis for hoping that 70 countries could do it now when advances in transportation and communication have brought nations closer together than the colonies were . . .

Tessa wrote,

I believe . . . the principal issue in postwar planning is whether another attempt shall be made to center force in national states or nonuniversal units, or whether it shall become the monopoly of a world organization . . .

Julian wrote,

This war is really only a result of the settlement after the last war, when what might have been a successful plan was defeated at the start by pet prejudices, jealousies, lust for revenge, and negligence. Public opinion stepped in to form a peace which in content was worse than many of the 19th century treaties . . .

Walt wrote,

I wonder if today we are trying to be "escapist" and making ourselves believe that there will never be any future wars. Maybe it is true that we are living in a more civilized world than a thousand or five hundred or even a hundred years ago; but in the standard of wars it seems to bog down quite a lot . . .

But there was an unexpected outcome of the animated discussion, the independent statements of positions. The group found itself stressing differences, spending energies on matters over which it disagreed. Through infrequency of mention, the group unconsciously minimized the fundamentals on which it was in agreement; for instance, the importance of fostering the democratic way of life, opposition to racism and imperialism, human welfare-centered values, the importance of a lasting peace. This encouraged the individualist who enjoyed the intellectual exploitation of differences. It did not allow sufficient opportunity for students within the class to learn to reconcile points of view, to learn to advance common concerns. How could we pull our thinking together; how could we reach group conclusions based on the inevitable process of give-and-take that characterizes social change?

We decided to take the last four weeks of our ten to meet in small groups, hammer out conclusions, and present them to the class as a whole. The effort would be to find common ground to stand upon; should there be some areas of irreconcilable difference, individuals were to be free to render minority reports. This latter, we agreed, was to be a last resort, after an individual had made his case and his concessions and could compromise no further without doing violence to basic convictions. As one of the students put it, if we couldn't get together with our common backgrounds of school and community experience, what hope could there be that peoples of many nations would achieve common understanding?

So had you visited the Ohio State University School in the spring of 1943 during a two week span, you would have found a group on Europe which pored over linguistic, economic, and political maps of Europe which were stretched across tables in the new social studies center. Under the chairmanship of the Austrian refugee, the seniors labored over the age-old questions of European boundaries, and over questions of economic integration of a nationally fragmented continent. Seated on the sofas and sprawled on the floor of the home economics living room, a group dealing with Asia talked out recommendations, conscious that racial issues and rising nationalisms were central to thought about the Orient. Stella, who left Hawaii after the murderous day at Pearl Harbor, served as group chairman; she had never ceased to marvel that it was in the continental United States that she had encountered racist thought and had to combat racist theory, topics seldom met in the racial melting pot of her

Islands. Making recommendations for American domestic policy attracted both the left and the right. More than any other students, these sweated over their self-imposed assignment to come together on reasonable agreements. Their able chairman was Tessa, daughter of an American Legion leader active in Americanism programs; both daughter and father learned much from Tessa's experience. In the classroom, a fourth committee met to make recommendations on international organization.

The groups were free to call on further sources of information. The group on Asia, for instance, listened to a recorded discussion by specialists who dealt with what should be done with Japan. When Ambassador Grew lectured in the city, students from the Asian group and members of the committee dealing with international organization were in his audience. But mostly the students talked out their ideas and reached consensus on statements of position which they set down.

By now many students had a respectable background for the attempt at recommendations. The lad most able to handle scholarly written materials had read by the close of the ten-week project:

Chase, Stuart. *The Road We Are Travelling*. New York: The Twentieth Century Fund. Pages 1-106. Total Book.

Chase, Stuart. *Goals for America*. New York: The Twentieth Century Fund, 1942. Pages 1-134. Total Book.

Streit, Clarence. *Union Now*. New York: The Macmillan Company, 1938. Pages 1-248. Total Book.

Hoover, Herbert and Gibson, Hugh. *The Problems of a Lasting Peace*. New York: Doubleday Doran and Company, 1942. Pages 1-288. Total Book.

Davis, Elmer, Editor, OWI. *Toward New Horizons*. Washington, D.C.: Government Printing Office, 1942. Pages 1-15.

Buell, Raymond Leslie. *Relations with Britain*, Fortune, May, 1942. Pages 1-12 (reprint).

Hansen, Alvin H. and Greer, Guy. *Toward Full Use of Our Natural Resources*, Fortune, November, 1942. Pages 1-10 (reprint).

Locke, Alain, Editor. "Color: Unfinished Business of Democracy." *Survey Graphic*. November, 1942. Pages 1-110.

Dean, Vera M. *The Struggle for World Order*. New York: The Foreign Policy Association, 1941. Pages 1-94.

Johnston, Eric. *The Road to Realism*. Washington. D.C.: Chamber of Commerce of the United States, 1943. Pages 1-10.

Chase, Stuart, Editor. "From War to Work," *Survey Graphic*, April, 1943. Pages 1-83.

Shirer, William L. *Berlin Diary*. New York: Simon and Schuster, 1940. Pages 1-605.

Hargrove, Marion. *See Here Private Hargrove*. New York: Henry Holt and Company, 1941. Pages 1-211.

It is interesting to contrast this student's emphasis on the printed page with the "bibliography" of another student who primarily used other techniques of learning. Included were mentions of OWI pamphlets, a Foreign Policy Headline Book, and miscellaneous magazine articles, but dominant were "discussions with my parents and friends," "weekly reading in *United States Weekly*," "daily reading in a New York City daily newspaper," "radio program 'The Man Behind the Gun' (every Sunday night)," "radio program 'Report to the Nation' (weekly)," and "an interview with a college dean."

One of the myths of modern education is the claim that laboratory school students are uniformly brilliant. From this stems the rationalization that the laboratory school experience is inapplicable to "normal" classes. Actually the ability span is often wider in the laboratory school. This wide ability span was characteristic of the group described. The academically weakest student in the class recorded as bibliography the following:

MOVIES: *The City, Edge of Darkness, Hitler's Children.*

PAMPHLETS:

Dean, Vera M. *The Struggle for World Order*. Foreign Policy Association, 1941. pp. 15, 38, 40, 58.

Stewart, Maxwell. *After the War*. pp. 10, 12, 13, 14, 16, 20.

Culbertson, Ely. "A System to Win the War," *Readers Digest*, April, 1943, 8 pages.

Johnston, Eric. *The Road to Realism*. Page 12.

Kirk, Grayson, and Sharp, Walter. *Uniting Today for Tomorrow*, Foreign Policy Association, New York: 1942, pp. 1-76.

"The Logic of the Air," *Fortune*, April, 1943, pp. 76-80, 188, 190, 192, 194, 196.

A student, representative of the middle group in the class, had read, in addition to Kirk and Sharp, Dean, Culbertson, Johnston, and two books by Chase mentioned above, the following:

Shotwell, James. *Commission to Study the Organization of the Peace, Second report, The Transitional Period*, February, 1942.

Office of War Information. *The Thousand Million*, 1943.

Bonnet, Henri. *The United Nations on the Way*. World Citizens Association, 1942.

After sufficient time for the meeting of minds, back to the class as a whole came the committees on Asia, Europe, American domestic economy, and international organization. They had mimeographed their recommendations, including occasional minority reports on specific items. In class meetings they read their recommendations, clarified their meanings rather than defended their conclusions, occasionally accepted modifications of phrasing suggested by the class, and offered their recommendations for a democratic vote. The results represented the best thinking which this group of high school seniors could do before the boys joined the armed services and the girls dispersed to summer jobs. Their recommendations were sent to Congressmen and a few others as the tentative conclusions of one of the numerous groups in America which had gathered to think together on the postwar world. ("Should we send it to Congressmen? After all we're just kids, not even voters." "That's right, but if we're old enough to fight, we're old enough to try to think.")

On Asia, the class accepted the following recommendations. In the light of "Asia policies" of the postwar years the judgment of these sixteen to eighteen-year-olds in 1943 may be of some interest. As the committee phrased it:

1. Manchuria should be given to China, and Japan eventually given "free access" to raw materials.
2. Make our educational facilities available for Chinese, Japanese, and Indians, and let the Americans who want to go over go over.
3. Japan should be policed for five to ten years, or as long as necessary.
4. England should give back Hong Kong.
5. Give India to Indians, everything but military power (until after the war).
6. Disarm China, Japan, and India and have an International Police Force.
7. China should be helped technically, but not politically.
8. Equal priority on seeds and farm machinery.
9. Remove all Japanese leaders. (This was rejected by the class and replaced by "Try, and punish Japanese leaders.")
10. Separate the Japanese government from the religion.
11. No exploitation of China and India. Missionaries and others go if asked, but not take control of cities.
12. Make it possible for China to export more than she imports by removing trade barriers and lowering tariffs.
13. To provide more jobs for the people we should make it possible to set up industry and manufacturing. (Therefore farmers who have not gone into industry will have more land and standard of living can be raised.)
14. Support all efforts to eliminate caste system and substitute a democratic philosophy.

On Europe the class ruled out, for voting purposes, an elaborate fifteen-point recommendation redrawing the map of Europe. The recommendation disposed not only of major countries but also assigned such dots on the map as Pantelleria, Helgoland, Luxembourg, and Zara to new-formed regional groupings. Staggered, the class pleaded ignorance. However, ten other recommendations were accepted.

Bob's minority recommendations carried in the class, though they hadn't with his committee. One indicated that the name League should not be applied to the European economic and social board. The other, marked by a closer vote, recommended that the proposed economic board be permanent and not temporary.

Via the minority report channel, one of Alex's favorite recommendations was adopted by the class by a narrow margin. "Recognizing that many of Europe's troubles are caused by the many diverse languages, I suggest that the teaching of Esperanto be made compulsory in all schools. Bilinguality in Europe will be an important factor in preserving a permanent peace."

In other committees too there were young people who made their cases and their concessions but who found irreconcilable differences where there could be no compromise without violence to basic value convictions. For instance, with respect to race, the majority of the committee recommended that there be education of all races to dispense with prejudice; prejudice within races should be abolished too; equal facilities for schooling; Southern Negroes go to separate schools until prejudice is lessened. A minority report strongly opposed this separate schools recommendation, which, however, was accepted by a narrow margin. The same minority won out on a recommendation that Negroes be employed at anything at which others are employed and lost on a recommendation that Negroes be allowed to live anywhere in America that any other people lived. Right or wrong, the class felt the minority report was an attempt to move too fast, without regard to long-established sectional attitudes, on America's problems of race relations.

The recommendations of the international organization group and the minority reports are too numerous for quotation in full here. The committee endorsed a league. A minority report extended the powers of the league to make it practically a world federation. Another minority report moved in the opposite direction, curtailing somewhat the power and centralization of the proposed league. The class finally endorsed a league as recommended by the committee and accepted a few international-minded amendments.

These, then, are some of the dreams the young men and women were dreaming in 1943. Before hard-headed practical men of affairs scoff, they might reflect on the results in world affairs and domestic economy of some decades dedicated to practicality, cynical of ideals and values. Munich was a product of the practical men. In the nation of the American dream, we have to take the long look down the road. We have to know where and why we're going, as well as learning the routes and the blockings along the way.

Nor is it the specific conclusions that are the most important outcomes of a study of problems. It is the process, not the product, that is basic to education. Eleanor Roosevelt, one of the many political leaders to whom the recommendations were sent, said well in a generous letter of acknowledgment, ". . . the important thing is that these young people are learning to think constructively and, though many of them may think differently in a few years, they have the ability to grow."

II
Learning Through Travel

The Background

EACH man discovers for himself what is already well-known. My rediscovery in my mid-twenties was social travel as a way of learning about people's lives in a geographical setting. Respectably equipped with an M.A. graduate degree and blessed for once with the opportunity to use a school teacher's long summer for travel, I went to Europe with my wife Bee. In 1936 we discovered foldboating, and cruised the Saar, Moselle, part of the Danube and Elbe rivers. Our longest cruise was 900 miles down the Danube River in 1937 through Germany, Austria, Czechoslovakia, Hungary and Yugoslavia. My cup overflowed when that legendary editor, Maxwell Perkins, mentor to Thomas Wolfe and F. Scott Fitzgerald, published my travel manuscript, *The Danube Flows Through Fascism*, through Scribner's.

In 1938 we cruised the Hudson River, the Rideau Canal in Canada, and the Connecticut River. For a 1939 American travel experience, we planned to join a 10,000-mile youth hostel trip combining train and bicycle across Canada and the United States.

But the best-laid plans of mice and men yield to parenthood and by the summer of 1939 Bee was caring for our first-born, Jon. My 10,000 mile hostel trip without her was the Indian summer of my social travel to learn the ways of people. Fall came fast in 1939 as Hitler's panzer divisions knifed into Poland and the long dark winter for social travelers set in and persisted throughout the world's bleakest years. My swan song was *Rolling Youth Hostel*, a travel manuscript permeated with an idea out of tune with the times: peace on earth, good will toward men. So nobody published it. I keep one copy made up of typed pages nicely bound. Maybe some friend will stop by my house and read it some day.

If Bee and I could live and learn so much through travel, couldn't high school youngsters learn from travel too? So social travel became one of the earliest of my enthusiasms in education; I fostered student travel during my near decade of teaching in the experimental Ohio State University School. We Americans are among the few people in the world who have full freedom to travel. Why not use our freedom to travel to educate our youth?

∾§ Here's how we found a way of travel that has stood us in good stead first as young marrieds and years later when we went to Europe with our children. That strange hybrid of canoe and kayak, the fold-boat, has helped us to get inside Europe and, more important, get inside the lives of European people. These are the opening pages of The Danube Flows Through Fascism.

4 *Railroads and Rivers*

FOR two weeks in the early summer of 1936 Bee and I played the game that is played yearly by increasing thousands of our countrymen, "Americans Touring Europe." We didn't like the pastime; you work too hard and give too much for what little you get.

Dutifully we gawked at the prim English countryside and in London visited St. Paul's, Westminster Abbey, the Tower, and Piccadilly Circus. We crossed the channel, saw all the correct things to see in Amsterdam, then, wondering why we had come, entrained southward into Germany.

Cologne was a typical episode in our brief fling at the tourist game. Through the sun-fondled hours of the day we jolted in a third-class carriage from the Holland border. The heat was intense and our fellow passengers zealously determined to prevent any foul seepage of fresh air into the train. Nobody spoke. Germans either begin to eat immediately upon entering a train or fall asleep, we noticed.

Across the aisle the silver Rhine ribbon stretched back to Holland. More often it hid behind the craned heads of sandwich consumers or dodged behind the octopus slums that embrace any railroad needling through any nation.

It was late afternoon as we staggered, smudged and tired, bearing a valise, duffel bag, and knapsack along platform B under the soot-stained glass arch of the Cologne Terminal. Outside the station a fringe of porters and taxi-drivers descended upon us. To them we were prey, not people. We were a legitimate way in which the fringe could earn a living.

"No, thanks, we're not ready yet. No thanks, they're not heavy. No, thanks. No. No."

Eenie, meeny, miney, mo. Where a Waldorf-Astoria at Mills Hotel rates? Where the Municipal Tourist Information Office with its flock of tourists asking where, when, how much? Momentarily we dropped the bags and stood gratefully lightened.

"That's the most beautiful cathedral in Europe," said Bee without much enthusiasm.

"Yeah," I said. "No, thanks." I saw the spires through a red blur of fatigue and perplexity.

Weaselface came along at that moment. "English I speak good because many years I am the New Yorker. A good fine cheap hotel by the 'bahnhof,' for you and your wife, yes?" We and the bags followed him. Five blocks, then an alley, then a study in dilapidation. Our hotel. A tip, a smirk bestowed upon Uncle Shylock.

Two hours of sleep revived us and we went out to see Cologne. Red mist no longer hung over the cathedral. We walked and looked; we stopped and drank beer. We found no opportunity to talk with any one; no one found an opportunity to talk with us. We were lonely visitors, like scores of foreigners in crowded cities.

"So," said disillusioned Bee from behind the beer foam, "we left our happy home for this. I'll bet the railroads are glad we came. They'll declare a special dividend by autumn."

"That's all right with me," I said. "What I object to is that we're not getting what we came for. We're having a little less fun per day than usual; we're getting filled to the gills with venerable monuments and things; and we're not finding out anything about what people are thinking and what's going on in the countries."

The next day we lugged our bags to the train and paid for our jolts. "How did you like Cologne?" people asked us in America months later. "It was very pretty," we said lamely. There wasn't much else we could say about it.

But overnight we changed worlds. We dropped the shuttling tourist game, tried and found wanting, and timidly entered into river sport. Though we didn't know it then, we were through forever with traditional tourism.

We crept by a wheezing local into the Saar, a region that swaps owners with every war, and at an ancient river town Paul and Janet Weinandy, friends who had preceded us over the frantic Atlantic, were waiting for us. Together we four hot-footed to the railroad freight office which yielded up the treasure that Bee and I had brought from America and sent through Europe to little Saarburg.

"We've got ours set up already," said Janet and Paul proudly.

Our treasure was bizarre, crammed into two canvas sacks, one high as man and wide as a rafter, the other squat and oblong, and both strapped to a pygmy wagon with two miniature wheels. The Germans who passed us as we wheeled the contraption through the streets to the river recognized a native product and wasted no astonishment on us.

On the banks of the Saar, beside the town wash that lay dry-ing on the green lawn, the sacks were dumped and from them streamed a six-yard strip of silver-colored rubber and more than a score of smooth yellow sticks and angular staves and thin boards. We pieced some of the dizzying variety of sticks together to make two frail-looking frameworks and inserted them into the rubber skin. Slowly the chaos took on shape. We added more assorted lumber. In a half hour a folding boat eighteen feet long, a silver sheath decked over fore and aft by blue fabric and with a cockpit large enough to seat two people, lay beside the River Saar. She was joined by her sister ship, the gleaming new folding boat—*faltboot* in German—that the Weinandys had bought days before. After a brief stay in old Saarburg two silver slivers manned by two captains and two first mates burbled through the rapids of the Saar toward the Moselle.

Life was better to us on the Saar and Moselle rivers than it had been in the two tourist weeks. After the sun had gripped his

55

foothold in the sky we would set our compromise between a canoe and a kayak on a float and pack into it the single knapsack that we had brought to the guesthouse the night before. Tenderly we would lift our home-sweet-home into the water and eddy and idle downstream. Ruined castles, watching for long-dead enemies, would menacingly glare down the river.

"The walls of Bernkastel were leveled by Louis XIV of France," Paul would say. "He wanted to rid France forever of the German peril. Even today in this valley many people hate France for the destruction of the Moselle castles more than for her victory in World War I."

Other lightly clad kayakers would paddle up to us and call the international river greeting, "Ahoy!" Sometimes we would pull in our paddles, hold all our boats together side by side, and drift and talk and sing while we let the current make what nautical decisions it would. As castles and towns edged gently around the bends, the other canoeists would ask us what it was like in America and tell us what it was like in Germany. Sometimes we'd meet Englishmen, Irishmen, Austrians.

Noon would come and we'd pull the boat out of the stream and leave it under the town bridge and go into the village with fifty cents for lunch and the wine of the region. We'd wander and stretch our legs and gape at the gabled, half-timbered houses and the peasants who took us for natives in our careless river clothes. Then the river again, for around the corner the new and unexpected lay, friends with an excoriation or eulogy of fascism, or peasant songs from the vineyards, or a beach for a swim, or a train jammed with people waving and envious of our indolence.

When the burden of red and gold got too heavy for the sun to carry and it began to drop behind the quilt of grapevines on the hills, we would travel only as far as the next town. From our river vantage point we would shop critically for an inn and choose the best garden on the Moselle, or the quaintest roof, or the newest, shiniest guesthouse. A float set out by "mein" host of the inn to catch the *faltboot* trade would be our landing place, and soon our boats would be perched for the night on wooden arms in a great hall filled with kayaks, and our knapsacks would sprawl on the floor of clean simple bedrooms, and we would be ensconced in the garden over a plaid tablecloth with food and clear yellow wine from the vined hills that rose behind us.

Sometimes after supper we would climb to the inevitable shattered castle brooding over the town from a hill crest, and later pick our way carefully down, talking of the thin river streak or ebbing sun or pitchy dungeon we had seen. Sometimes we were content to stay and make new friends in the medieval public rooms of taverns where the wainscoted walls were garlanded with kettles, pistols, steins, copper platters, swords, and jugs.

"Ah, from America! And sportsmen!" said the Germans. The welcome was on the doormat. We had a status; we weren't just prey. And that's what our way of travel gave to us—the opportunity to become a part of the life that was going on around us, the opportunity to be more than spectators at a pageant with scenery and costumes. We belonged.

Now let anything try to divorce us from our companion in intimate exploration, the fifty-seven-pound folding boat that can float along continental arteries like a disengaged pond lily. We've found our game, our method of indulging an insatiable curiosity about people and social institutions on an income distinctly more limited than that of Croesus or Ford.

ॐ *I first experienced youth hosteling when we cruised the Connecticut River by foldboat as chronicled in* Foldboat Holidays, *an anthology by enthusiasts, some white water adventurers, others, like ourselves, leisurely cruisers. We thought hosteling a wonderful idea, too little recognized in America.*

The possibilities in hostel travel for all American youth have never ceased to intrigue me. Hostel Vacation *summarizes the enormous potentiality this way of travel holds. The late Beardsley Ruml espoused a similar idea (it was in the air) in* Coronet.

The potentiality has never been realized in America. In Europe, 1,400,000 young people go hosteling each year. On April 20, 1960, the New York Times *reported that "Japan is following the European craze for youth hostels. In nine years, the movement here has gathered a membership of 80,000 and opened almost 300 hostels."*

In America there are only 15,000 hostelers. American youth aspires to four-wheeled status symbols, high tail-finned living rooms complete with radio, foam-rubber comfort, complete privacy, and high mobility. Traveling under your own steam encounters too tough—or should we say too soft?—competition.

I am reminded of the time a few years ago in Nashville, Tennessee, when a self-appointed critic of the schools, an automobile dealer, inveighed against "soft" modern education. Fremont Wirth, historian, responded with an ironic rebuttal condemning modern automobiles which have deprived youth of the use of their legs, eliminated the stern discipline of getting out and getting under, sabotaged thrift through installment buying, destroyed parental control through extensive cruising range, encouraged immorality through lovers' lanes and passion pits, etc. Whose fault? The automobile dealers'!

5 *Hostel Travel*

HOSTELING is a way of travel. It's a way of travel for the hiker, the biker, the canoeist who travels under his own steam. It's a way for young Americans who want to see the world they inhabit. It's a way that gives youth without wealth a key which unlocks a world that formerly was the private preserve of the privileged.

What is youth hosteling? Monroe Smith, the founder of American Youth Hostels, once told me, "It's so beautiful and simple that some people can't understand it." For a hostel is just an overnight accommodation where the hosteler may stay after a day on the trail, a place where farm folk or urban dwellers adopt him for the night. A hosteler is someone young in heart— four to ninety-four in age—who speeds downhill on two wheels and clatters noisily over covered bridges, who walks the silent trails while the sun swings overhead in a giant arc, who paddles his way through rips or lets the river current carry him toward the sea. Hosteling is just a way of traveling to have fun.

Yet hosteling is more than travel at a dollar a day. It's more than big muscle activity. It's more than a glimpse of the world from a flying bike; it's more than absorption in the spectacle nature stages for mankind.

For hosteling can help to build the democratic way of life, that way of life which is the American creed, the American commitment. In hosteling, the traveler meets a variety of other fellows. The pullman traveler meets pullman travelers. The auto traveler brings his own comfortable little world along with him, and glasses himself in to make his isolation still more complete. But the hosteler meets the office girl on her week's vacation as well as the young college man. Some whom he meets go to temples and some to weather-beaten frame churches, and some exercise the time-honored prerogative of going to no church at all. Some are Johnnies-come-lately to America and some boast ancestors who came over on the badly overcrowded Mayflower. Some whom he meets may be French or Greek or Chinese or Russian or Scotch. To those who go down the trail together, who try new folk dances at the hostel, who create bizarre breakfasts with raw oatmeal as a base, who work on their holidays to build better hostels, the differences can be unimportant. It's the common experiences that count. As hostelers, all are deeply engaged in one of man's oldest activities, having fun. They're sharing the same traditions, customs, enthusiasms, boredoms. Kinship feeds on sharing. Stereotypes break down when the other fellow, engaged in an enterprise with you, turns out to be a human being, too. Suspicion flourishes only in an atmosphere where the other fellow is not known.

Hosteling is no magic panacea. Hosteling alone will never build unity or prevent wars. But it is one of the weapons in the arsenal of democracy for building a world marked by understanding. Hosteling is ever an opponent of hostility.

Through an initial experience, hosteling close to home, the high school youth would wet his travel feet. With his group he would plan a trip to get better acquainted with his own country and state. Traveling the youth hostel way, bicycling, walking, skiing, horseback riding, or canoeing, he would visit his neighbors at work and play. He would not rush along looking at a blurred landscape and blank spaces. He would travel in a more leisurely way, taking time to visit with people—to know and understand them. For fundamentally it is the quality of the experience that counts, not the mileage covered. While he learned the thrill of a new trail, he would cook his own meals, make his own bed, wash his own dishes, and improve his own hostel. He would learn things about his community and region which he never knew existed.

His second travel experience would take him from his own area to a region miles away. Leaving his train, he would go hosteling again as one of a group under skilled leadership. He would stop nights at farm houses or in simple quarters, spend his days in biking or hiking down side roads to observe lumberjacks or fishermen, to visit factories or mills or power plants. Without realizing that he was getting a "lesson," he would learn that though people a thousand miles away may be "different," they're more kin than quaint. In two weeks on the trail at home and another two weeks on the trail in a region new to him, he would discover much of the marvelous diversity that is America, while learning to get along with others.

Unless trips are subsidized by schools, the state, or private philanthropy, there will be fewer young Americans who can have the crowning American experience, the transcontinental trip. A "rolling youth hostel trip" combines reduced-fare train travel with hiking and biking in many regions. It's the chance for the Bostonian to see the Pacific Northwest, for the Georgian to become acquainted with Minnesota's folkways—not travel so that our youth may gape like tourists at historical markers or the Capitol dome but a basic introduction to the varied cultures and the economic life of the country. It is travel which fosters identification of self with fellow citizens, for patriotism can't be learned out of books or from listening to one's elders. Patriotism is the insight and devotion that grows out of mixing with and understanding people.

For a fourth travel experience, hosteling spans the seas. Some of our high school youth, fortified by native travel experiences, could become ambassadors of good will to the youth of other countries. Might they not go as unostentatious social travelers, sportsmen who partake of the life of the country through biking its roads, foldboating its rivers, hiking its trails? There's a "belongingness" which one can achieve the hostel way but which is barred to the ordinary tourist scattering largess.

A dream? Of course it's a dream, but all the things in life we prize grew from dreams.

There would appear to be two possible paths along which we might go as we try to broaden hosteling travel for high school youth. We might turn to the government and work for a student travel agency in the tradition of the CCC or NYA. We might experimentally foster hosteling experiences in certain American schools and communities and let success infect others with the potentialities.

Recourse to central government is the usual pattern of the man in a hurry. But good education can all too seldom be achieved simply by fiat or edict. The need for leadership training for social travel persists; the problem of consent continues; the need for controlled experimentation remains; antagonism to central government by a large segment of the public, including many educators, is real. Good hosteling, like good education, can result only from broad participation in planning, meeting the needs of individuals, adapting to localities and environments. If government is called upon, it must be for financial assistance and cooperation with grass roots efforts, rather than for provision of a mass production travel plan, mechanically perfect as a robot.

If we had a central school authority in this country, we might turn to it, but none exists in the American system nor is likely to exist. Our education, for better or worse, is highly localized. School and community needs differ in American life; curricula vary; the readiness and equipment of school men to foster programs of social travel reflect unequal levels of development. In America, no master plan may be clamped down upon schools.

Inevitably then, our hope for realization of the hostel dream must rest primarily with experimentation in the schools. It must rest with the vision and leadership of the pioneering schools, those which are experimental in philosophy, concerned for continual improvement of the educative process. Such schools might experiment with the first step described above, hostel travel in the school's own locality. It is not inconceivable that some might embrace all four stages in their program. Experimentation would be greatly encouraged could there be a Social Travel Study which would help school people to develop know-how and leadership in this field. Such a study might foster trips in selected schools, carefully evaluate the result in terms of human growth, aid trip programs through supplying specialists who might share leadership, help to develop teachers competent to introduce young Americans to their nation through media other than books alone, let all concerned know of that which works and that which misses fire.

The vision of wide social travel for many American youth is still vision, not reality. Whether it is ever achieved depends upon willingness to experiment. Its fate, like the fate of all dreams in a democracy, rests upon the actions of you and me.

*⋙ I helped to initiate youth hosteling in Ohio and experimented
with it in my teaching. The hostel experience reported here took
place twenty years ago. I have left the closing paragraphs in the future
tense to suggest the anticipation of a young teacher. Today I need
only add that seldom have I felt more rewarded as an educator than
during the months of close rapport with students as a youth hostel
project was carried through at the Ohio State University School.*

6 Youth Hosteling in Ohio

In Columbus, the capital city of Ohio, there were some young
men and women who had an idea in common. At one time or
another each had said to himself, "Some day I'm going to do
something about hosteling in Ohio." Among the enthusiasts was
a newspaper man who called a meeting, as a trial balloon, through
the columns of his newspaper. They all came: the YMCA man
who saw youth hostels as a supplement to his biking program;
the assistant dean who had mapped a hiking trail through Ohio's
scenic hill country; the young couple who had hosteled in the
Great Smokies one unforgettable summer; the educator who
thought he saw a new channel through which youth might navi-
gate toward the American dream; the engineering student from
the East who had taught hostelers to ski; the publisher who
couldn't forget that it was the young who were a sizable percentage of the unemployed in a world they never made. And
there were others. We liked the purpose, "to promote a greater
knowledge, understanding and love of the world"; we formed a
Buckeye Trails District Committee of the American Youth
Hostels. Much of the leisure time that we could discover we
devoted to talking with the variety of key people concerned for

young people in the towns and cities of central Ohio. We helped them sponsor local committees charged with selection of hostels and houseparents; we addressed meetings of all descriptions, showed films, sent out releases and letters, raised money, planned and replanned, engaged in a welter of organizational activities. In a year, a loop consisting of five hostels stretched across the Buckeye country, and almost three hundred overnights were recorded in the Ohio hostel ledgers. The committee members had learned more of American life than they could measure.

The trip taken by students of the Ohio State University School illustrates some of the experiences other youngsters may encounter on hostel trips guided by educators. A group of ten, mostly of the tenth and eleventh grades in the school, traveled with teacher-leaders along Buckeye Trails for a week in September 1940, before the opening of the school year. Freshly, intimately, they explored among the human and natural resources of the state that has been called typically American. At the dairy farm hostel, while they cooperatively cooked their supper beside the Licking River, they talked about the debris from the spring flood still tangled in the trees overhead and of the erosion they had noticed which had leached gullies into the riverbanks. They left their bicycles beside the Ohio Canal, built in 1826, while they tried to recreate imaginatively the old Northwest of the days of the rifle, the axe and the bag of seed. In vivid contrast was the scientific hybrid seed corn farm that served for home-sweet-home next night. Here a friendly farmer-houseparent was ready to talk with any who might ask about Mendel's law in relationship to scientific agriculture. At night, before the hostelers sang, played country games and folk danced, they listened to an informal talk on ecology and Americana by a clerk in the local clothing store who knew more of the botany and geology of his beloved hills than did the professors he occasionally guided. Flat on the floor they pored over his annotated topographic map which was to be their guide next morning. As they hiked their sixteen miles, their bicycles temporarily abandoned, the trees were hued with premonitions of the reds and yellows of autumn; even the most self-consciously virile confessed to seeing beauty in the lattice-work of timbers crisscrossing on the sides of covered bridges. The group had many experiences: industries in the towns en route, the forest ranger-houseparent with his nature knowledge, the extravagant geology of the cave district, the tall story competition about the fireplace, the most general of all general stores where William Moore cut hair on Thursday afternoons and over the counter at a penny a piece sold his postcards of the McKinley-Bryan campaign exactly as he had in his spryer days. Throughout the trip the hostelers made their own beds, cleaned up the hostel, bought and cooked their meals in scheduled crews. The trip cost was $66.93 for the ten for a week, less than a dollar a day per individual.

Hostel work holidaying is another possibility that might be utilized for educational ends by the energetic in our profession. Twice during the summer of 1940, members of a class in education and of the first Workshop of Ohio University at Athens drove to the Lancaster hostel. They met there vacationing students from Ohio State and graduates and students of the University School who had come to the hostel on their own initiative and who had already begun a work holiday. The combined human energy of teachers-in-service and of young students was directed to converting an old summer kitchen into a livable hostel. Piled-up litter vanished; walls were whitewashed or painted; AYH guide triangles for trails were made; a floor was laid; firewood was cut; brooms came into play. Curtains were made in the Ohio University Workshop in the interim between visits

The enthusiasm of the summer hostelers and workers has swept into the academic year now under way at the University School. As part of a community and regional study begun in a core course, the eleventh-graders plan to collaborate with young people throughout the state and with the adults on hostel committees in carrying on the youth hostel idea. This idea was sponsored by the youngsters who were on the September trip. In the light of plans recently made it appears that the group will focus on improving the existing hostels partially through work in the field, partially through use of school laboratories; they will collaborate on the establishment of a local hostel and summarize the results of their community-regional survey for the use of those

65

of their contemporaries who visit the towns and cities and rolling lands of Ohio as they travel the youth hostel way.

Hosteling is one way in which educators can promote the democratic way of life, fostering the optimal development of individuals through widening the area of shared interests and continuously utilizing the method of intelligence.

ᵛᔒ Persuaded of the educational value of social travel, the Ohio State University School sponsored short trips for all grade levels and sustained trips for juniors and seniors. This account of a junior-class trip emphasizes the process of planning. The supposedly "small" details of cooperative trip planning make or break social travel.

What an opportunity for realistic education student-planned social travel affords! The possibilities for study of community problems are immense.

7 Youth Visits Industrial Detroit

IF A visitor had happened to enter a certain room in Ohio State University School on a Friday morning in January, he might have thought that he had blundered into a convention of youthful local boosters, every individual intent on vaunting his own city. But after the visitor had listened a few moments, he would have become further confused, because topics were mentioned which good local boosters shun. A speaker contended, "Detroit has slums and we could study housing there," and met a quick response, "But Washington has slums almost in the shadow of the White House, and we could get a housing administrator to talk to us." The eleventh grade students were trying to decide which city would make the most profitable trip for them, given their present needs, interests, and program of study. The discussions and projected trip were part of orientation, a program of study and experience in the eleventh and twelfth grades of the Ohio State University School.

Don, the junior class president who presided over the weekly session of class business during orientation, banged his gavel and ruled that each city be taken up in turn. "Washington, D.C." Students who were favorably inclined pointed out that here was a trip with an emphasis on government, and couldn't everyone see that one of the most important things in American life was government? Couldn't they see from this year's study of the American scene in social science that government was steadily extending its activities and would probably continue to extend them even further in the future? Didn't government account for a great number of occupations, many of the occupations which we will go into? We could visit—and a long list of possibilities spilled out.

In the same manner, Detroit, an industrial automobile city, and Pittsburgh, an industrial steel city, were analyzed. A trip that would combine government and industrial emphasis—to Washington with a stopover at Pittsburgh—found proponents, largely those who had supported the Pittsburgh idea earlier. One persuasive voice was raised for Philadelphia, "an unspecialized, all-around city like our own city where most of us will work." A small lobby of well-informed intellectuals advocated a southern regional trip through the Tennessee valley. What an opportunity, they argued, to study a newer pattern of life and work in America, the TVA! Each group of advocates had investigated costs through phone calls, letters, and conversations with bus companies, railroads, hotels, and traveled acquaintances.

On a student suggestion, the president appointed a committee to write to parents for advice. A letter was prepared with two appended pages of information describing the range of trips and purposes. The committee that framed the letter tabulated the responses. There was no decided preference, though Washington or Detroit ranked highest in the parents' replies. The class plunged into a final consideration of relative values.

Detroit was selected on two counts. The major one was a genuine desire to study how men live and work in modern industrial America, and to become more familiar with the conflict between labor and capital. The minor one was that the trip was less expensive.

Once the Detroit decision had been reached after two ballots, the class president wasted no time on meandering discussion. He and the class and the general chairman for the Detroit trip, who was immediately elected from among many nominees, knew how efficient the committee method could be when working for a tangible accomplishment. Hadn't every party, dance, and other social event been planned and carried out by student committees? Wasn't working with a variety of committees an integral part of education as they had experienced it?

"What committees do we need?" A democratically planned trip moved into the most important stage, arrangements.

A transportation committee was needed to determine whether bus or train should be used and to arrange for safe and cheap travel.

A committee on trips within Detroit had extremely important work in prospect—to arrange by letters for all visits, to schedule a balanced program, to arrange exact time and other basic details with plants and speakers after we arrived in Detroit.

An entertainment committee was suggested to plan a balanced program of diversified recreation, with allowance for sufficient rest and sleep.

A hotel and food committee was needed to arrange for inexpensive material comfort.

A finance committee was to have as its function setting an exact minimum cost, collecting money in prearranged installments to meet group needs for transportation and hotel, coordinating the financing of other committees.

An agreements committee was instituted to set up standards of behavior.

A new parent-student committee was formed to continue the work of the committee which wrote home for advice on the most valuable trip. Its function was to keep parents informed on all developments in planning.

From a flood of volunteers the trip chairman selected committee members. Sometimes he chose a reticent person seldom seen on committees; the experience would be good for him. Sometimes he selected a recognized responsible leader; if the committee bogged down, the leader would save it. Sometimes he disregarded the mute plea of a hand. "You're on the party committee already." Sometimes he selected a close friend so that the chairman could check up informally on committee progress; the chairman knew he had a man-sized job.

Twenty-five out of forty-one students were on active responsible committees. A group decision was that committees were to proceed as far as they could, short of final decisions, that they were to write letters or phone as necessary, then recommend to the whole group. Final decisions were to be authorized by the whole group after a committee report had been heard and approved.

Letters were written to the prominent Detroit hotels. Delegated students visited transportation agencies after school. The committee on agreements pondered specifications. Students named the faculty members whom they wished to invite and asked the administration to select advisers from their list. The committee on trips in Detroit winnowed, with the aid of the whole group, three days of educational activity from a compiled list of twenty-six possibilities. The purposes of the trip became still more sharply defined in all minds and some phases were discarded as possible of duplication in Columbus. What survived were essentially salient aspects of life and work in an industrial automobile city marked by conflict between labor and capital.

The teacher compiled a bibliography for optional reading before the Detroit trip. Books were listed under headings—industrial, labor, our economic system, and novels. That students might survey many points of view, the authors were classified as conservative, liberal, or radical, and the words were carefully defined in a footnote.

Ten students decided that they would not go to Detroit, largely because of financial reasons. During March, these students held their own meetings and planned a "little Detroit trip" to take place in Columbus while their classmates were away.[1]

[1] When the Educational Policies Commission of the National Education Association and the American Association of School Administrators reported this junior class trip to Detroit in *Learning the Ways of Democracy,* the Commission added, "The following year, when the class as seniors planned to visit New York City, the problem of economic selection was vigorously attacked. The group raised money through class projects. Earnest discussions followed on what was the democratic thing to do with the money raised, and with the unnamed people who couldn't afford to pay all the costs of the trip. Should the group money be divided equally among all? Should the group money be used by those who needed additional assistance if they were to undertake the trip?

In February the parent-student committee dispatched the following letter home:

The Junior Class this year has planned to go to Detroit. The general purpose of our trip is to study life in an industrial city. We plan to stop at Toledo to see a glass factory, which is a subsidiary of the Ford Motor Company. In Detroit, we intend to visit the Ford plant, the Chrysler plant, the General Motors Research Laboratory, Greenfield Village, art galleries, museums, and housing projects.

We will hear representatives of the Ford and Chrysler motor companies, a speaker for the United Automobile Workers Union, a representative of the government on the relations between industry and labor. We believe a discussion of student problems in which Detroit students would participate could be very valuable to us.

The trip, however, will not be all work, for we plan to take an excursion to Canada and will also have some of the evenings for theatres and other forms of amusement.

Each afternoon of the four day trip, students returned to the hotel early enough for baths and a rest; then in the hour before dinner they wrote answers to questions on scientific aspects of the day's experiences and on social aspects:

What is research and how does a large corporation handle this aspect of modern industry?

Do new ideas encounter hostility in research? Do new ideas encounter hostility in fields other than research?

How does a worker's job in a mass production industry, like the automobile industry, differ from a worker's job in an establishment like Seagraves or Jeffries, which specialize in individual orders or custom built products?

Social-economic implications of each possibility were worked out in class discussions. The students finally adopted the following plan. They determined the total cost of transportation and hotel for the group. Each person contributed toward this pool, as best he could, an amount known only to the teacher. Most paid in the average amount. Some paid in more. Some paid in less. All money raised by class activities went into the pool. The treasurer used the total sum to pay for transportation and hotel. Beyond this each individual paid personally for his own food and recreation, and varying sums of money, of course, were spent. Through such an arrangement all who wished to could go on the New York City trip; yet no one was completely subsidized."

Accidents and insecurity in old age are two problems which workers have. Why should the Chrysler Corporation have a department devoted to getting rid of accidents, and not have a department devoted to getting rid of insecurity in old age?

Describe how the Chrysler people plan production of Chrysler cars. Should there be some great organization to coordinate the plans of each company and to plan all American production with equal care? Opinion.

Compare the Chrysler visit to the Ford visit in regard to jobs of workers, company attitude toward labor or unionism, the reception of visitors.

What do the displays at the Ford Museum attempt to portray? If you could change the arrangement of the Museum, what would you change?

After returning to University School, the individuals who comprised the Detroit and Columbus groups exchanged notes and ideas in several discussion sessions. The Detroit group rewrote and improved answers to questions and reworked their diaries of Detroit experiences.

Nine months later, while planning for a senior trip, the group formally evaluated the visit to industrial Detroit. Two comments by students may well serve as a summary of the value of trip experiencing as students see it.

One wrote:

"I think trips are loads of fun. This doesn't mean that I don't think they are educational too. It is because they are fun that we learn so much. Everything that we saw and heard during our trip was experienced in pleasant surroundings and came to us in a form that didn't seem like work. Thus we were more ready to listen and think about it. This experience and gathered knowledge will probably remain with us for the rest of our lives. . . ."

Another explained:

"The main thing I got out of the Detroit trip was the ability to see two sides to labor and governmental questions. After seeing myself what is good and bad in labor unions I can draw my own conclusions much better. . . ."

III
Laughing
at
Ourselves

The Background

CHANGING the curriculum is like moving a cemetery. Until you try it, you have no idea how many friends the dead still have.

I had the opportunity to work at changing the curriculum nationally in the mid-nineteen forties. After nine years of teaching at University School along with studying for my doctorate at Ohio State University, I worked with organizations emphasizing problem areas for study by all high school students, such as consumer education and intercultural education.

The Consumer Education Study was a project of the National Association of Secondary School Principals, a department of the National Education Association. The Better Business Bureau supplied the funds for the development of consumer education in American schools and scrupulously eschewed any controls. Thomas H. Briggs, a retired professor and the able Study director, supplied the basic idea, that one most effectively brought the learning experiences of youngsters up-to-date by developing textbooks for them. My contribution was writing *Time on Your Hands* and *Economic Roads for American Democracy*, two Consumer Education Study textbooks for high school students.

When I became director of publications and learning materials for the Bureau for Intercultural Education, a privately financed, philanthropically supported agency fostering better human relations among Americans of varied colors, creeds, and nationality backgrounds, I brought with me the realization that there were many other ways to skin the curricular cat. Textbooks helped in making changes. But teacher education was needed too. So was consultation to school systems. So was a new approach to old subjects. We used them all at the Bureau. Consequently, my Bureau responsibility was to edit a magazine for teachers and textbooks for students, to write articles, yearbook chapters and resource units, and to cooperate with colleagues consulting with school systems.

In 1947 I became a full time professor at the University of Illinois. I had been a college professor of sorts earlier, for the post at University School had carried academic rank and I also had taught summers at universities across the country.

But a full time professorship was different from summer teaching. So was a full professorship. It meant that I could now cultivate my academic garden as a curriculum specialist as well as I knew how. It meant that I need not be upward mobile unless I wanted to be a dean, which I didn't. Professors define a dean as a man too smart to be a president but not smart enough to stay a full professor.

At Illinois I attempted to help undergraduates and graduate students to teach the social studies, served as a consultant to the state curriculum program, carried on research reported through more appropriate media than this book, and wrote a unit on intercultural education.

To write some light columns titled *The Importance of People* was a welcome change of pace for me after some years of serious professional writing.

The magazine that carried my columns was *Educational Leadership*, the monthly journal of the Association for Supervision and Curriculum Development of the National Education Association. ASCD is made up primarily of the second in command in school systems: the curriculum directors, the supervisors, some assistant superintendents.

Like popular magazines, professional journals of educators have their columnists. Sometimes they are solemn recorders of the current scene; sometimes they edit others' contributions. I chose to chuckle a bit, I hope not unkindly, at some of the foibles of my beloved profession. To me, freedom to laugh is the fifth freedom. If we Americans ever stop laughing at ourselves, we will be in a bad way.

⊷§ Immediately after publication of the following column, letters from readers suggested sacred and profane aspects of class stratification among the American Educators which had been carelessly overlooked by my anthropologist. People apparently enjoy elaborating on his classifications and you may too. When I have used the anthropologist's reflections as an introduction to talks at teachers' meetings, applications of the class structure of the American Educators to local conditions and celebrities have occasionally been overheard later in the lobby. Of course I deplore this. With apologies to my sociologist friends who pioneered a useful concept of social class and to superintendents who have vowed never again to unleash me on their speakers' platforms, I submit an off-beat analysis, The Remarkable Culture of the American Educators.

8 *The Remarkable Culture of the American Educators*

"FEW more fascinating cultures exist than that of the American Educators," said the anthropologist to his colleague.

The two anthropologists were deep in their favorite leather chairs at the Explorers' Club. They had been trading information on tribal customs they had found at the far ends of the earth. The roaring blaze in the great stone fireplace was fed steadily with massive logs. From the paneled walls, masks used in primitive ceremonials stared down unblinkingly.

"As you know," continued the speaker, "some of America's greatest anthropologists have applied the anthropological approach to American society as a whole. Others have studied isolated American sub-cultures, such as hill people of the Appalachians. But, until my study, occupational sub-cultures in modern America were uncharted anthropologically."

"How did you happen to choose the American Educators as the occupational sub-culture to be studied?"

"The same three standards I used in choosing South Seas cultures for inclusion in my recent book."

"Check my memory," said his companion, his eyes wandering to the primitive masks. "The tribe must have a special language for in-group communication."

"Right. The vocabulary and sentence structure of the upper class of the American Educators are particularly remarkable."

"The tribe must manifest characteristic in-group behavior."

"Right again. In local communities the American Educators, except for their gregarious upper-middle class, are regarded as strange and special creatures. This, along with the rituals of their upper class, may help explain the absorption of the American Educators in talking to themselves through manuscripts, magazines, and meetings."

"Third, the tribe must be suspicious of the out-group."

"Remarkable memory! 'Lay public' is the word this culture uses for the out-group. Roughly translatable as 'foreigners.' "

His companion lit a pipe. "You mentioned classes among the American Educators. What is their class system?"

"As a fellow anthropologist, you are of course familiar with the five (sometimes six) social classes documented by many able students of American society. A disreputable lower-lower class. A poor but honest upper-lower class. A solid, substantial lower-middle class. An energetic, influential upper-middle class. A prestige-bearing, established upper class. Approximately so, Herbert?"

"Over-simplified by you for the purpose of summary, of course."

The student of life among the American Educators leaned forward earnestly and tapped his listener's knee as he continued. "Herbert, I have made a tremendous discovery. The American Educators have an *educational* class system which parallels the *social* class system of their country!"

"How does one recognize an upper class American Educator?" asked Herbert, thoughtfully blowing pipe smoke at a particularly hideous tribal mask. "Upper *educational* class, that is."

"I found the habitat of the upper class American Educators in the universities," responded the anthropologist enthusiastically. "Here the member of the upper educational class weaves elaborate theories, engages in research, initiates acolytes to the upper class, produces tomes, and disputes the findings of other members of the upper class. It is believed in this class that the more incomprehensible the language and the fewer the readers, the more the result is to be judged profound and thus worthy of respect. Over the years, knowledge gathered by the upper class trickles down to the masses. The cultural lag is estimated at fifty to seventy-five years.

"The upper educational class is separated from the other classes by an extraordinary caste-like barrier termed Ph.D. and Ed.D. But so honorable is this caste-like distinction that it is now almost a requirement for upper-middle class membership. The upper educational class is in great demand for ceremonial occasions such as local institutes and state meetings required of the lower-lower and upper-lower educational classes."

"And on these occasions the upper class speeches change the behavior of these lower classes?"

"Of course not," said the student of American Educators indignantly. "Not even the upper-middle and lower-middle classes in charge of the meetings expect change to result. The upper class member is there to grace the meeting with upper class participation. I *said* these were ceremonial occasions!"

"Of course. And the other classes?"

"The upper-middle educational class," continued the enthusiastic anthropologist, "is populated largely by people high in the public school hierarchy. It also includes a few declassed university professors who have been revealed as upper-middles in upper's robes, and a handful of teachers from highly rated experimental schools. They are vigorous, energetic, and gregarious characters. They are also distinguishable by their many griefs about something they call 'the curriculum.' This curriculum (which, frankly, I don't quite understand) must be in a very bad way, for they are constantly doing things to it. Indeed, the upper-middle class holds annual tribal gatherings in which they pray over this curriculum affair!"

"Do the two lower classes pray at these meetings too?"

"No," said the investigator. "One of the major educational class distinctions between the middle classes and the lower classes is in this matter of meeting. The lower classes do not attend such gatherings on the sea coast of New Jersey or in the metropolis or salubrious mountains. The few lower class members who do attend are definitely upward mobile. Incidentally, one important distinction between the upper-middle educational class and the lower-middle educational class is that the upper-middle educational class has expenses paid to these tribal gatherings while lower-middle does not. Consequently, the lower-middle class is much more frequently encountered in state meetings.

"Degree of literacy also appears to be a distinction between the two middle classes. The upper-middle class contributes to magazines and yearbooks; the lower-middle class does not write for publication."

"You mentioned economic considerations. Is the upper class much more prosperous than the upper-middle educational class?"

The explorer of the folkways of the American Educators was genuinely shocked. "Indeed not! Surely, Herbert, you know that money isn't an infallible index to social position. The way one's culture *regards* one is important. Reputation! Many upper-middles have been known to give up crass material advantages to join the uppers in university meccas. Similarly, when some uppers have shifted their class position to upper-middle, income was gained but face was lost."

"And the lower classes?" asked Herbert, watching the primitive masks through narrowed eyes. He had the illusion that they were winking at him.

"The upper-lower educational class is made up of garden variety Educators who are regarded as the backbone of the American Educator tribe. All of the class members above them admire and extol upper-lowers. However, none wishes to be one again. The upper-lowers attend workshops, take courses, try experiments, study child development, serve on committees, keep anecdotal records. They try to interpret what the three classes above them advocate. This is no easy task as you can plainly see. When an upper-lower achieves a fine interpretation, the upper-middles or an upward mobile lower-middle generously translate it back into the special tribal language at the tribal gatherings.

Yes, upper-lowers are quite different from lower-lowers—" He shuddered.

"Yes?"

"On one thing all of the other educational classes are agreed. They deplore the attitudes and behavior of the lower-lower educational class. As a matter of fact, the uplift of the lower-lowers is the major work of the middle classes. The middle classes try to make upper-lowers out of lower-lowers. Lower-lowers resist all new and educationally moral ideas. They simply put in their time. They have a peculiar unofficial slogan, 'Friday, thank God.' They are not upward mobile. One informant refers to them as the Dead End Kids of American education. Apparently they have few middle class virtues."

"A remarkable culture," said Herbert.

"Let me illustrate," said the indefatigable anthropologist. "Curriculum Director Joseph Doakes, who is lower-middle educational class, plans to attend a convention of an organization mysteriously initialed ASCD, which is basically upper-middle with some upper and some lower-middle members. Now Doakes. . . ."

On the paneled walls, the masks used in primitive ceremonials were smiling at each other.

᪥ The Ladder to Success in Universities *was really Harold Benjamin's idea, inspired by his own promotion from dean at Maryland to professor at Peabody. He even loaned me the literary use of that eminent savant who supposedly wrote* The Saber-Tooth Curriculum, *Professor J. Abner Peddiwell, Ph.D., Petaluma College. Can friendship be carried further? (Advt: McGraw-Hill—if Bobbs-Merrill will excuse the expression—has just reissued in a paperback form* The Saber-Tooth Curriculum, *a classic of educational humor which has been too long out of print. Beg, borrow, steal—even buy—a copy.)*

Ben and I are still waiting for a university to solve its promotion problems by adopting Peddiwell's eminently reasonable proposal. What are you Boards of Trustees waiting for?

9 *The Ladder to Success in Universities*

THE anthropologist looked disturbed as he sank into his favorite leather chair at the Explorers Club. He stared into the roaring blaze in the great stone fireplace. From the paneled walls, masks used in primitive ceremonials stared down unblinkingly.

Herbert, a fellow club member, eased his frame into the leather chair beside him. The anthropologist continued to look broodingly into the fireplace. Herbert decided to make conversation.

"How is your study of the remarkable culture of the American Educators coming along?" asked Herbert.

"Oh, hello," said the anthropologist. "Quite well, thank you. Till today."

"Yes?" said his companion encouragingly.

"You remember," said the anthropologist, "that I was studying the class structure of the American Educators. Educational class structure, that is. I set down the characteristics of the five identifiable classes: the grave and learned uppers, the gregarious

82

upper-middles, the expense-accountless lower-middles, the garden variety upper-lowers who are the backbone of the tribe, and the lower-lowers with their peculiar slogan, 'Friday, thank God!' My researches dealt with considerations of occupational status and social mobility. My studies led me into related fields. Recently I have been investigating the ladder to success in universities. That is where I encountered a difficulty today."

"Why should that prove difficult?" asked Herbert. "The ladder to success in universities seems plain. On the bottom rung of the ladder is the overworked, underpaid graduate assistant. The lowly fellow tabulates statistics, teaches courses no one else wants to teach, marks papers, takes graduate work, and wrestles with his dissertation."

Musingly, the anthropologist interjected, "The last form of legalized slavery remaining in the United States."

"Naturally," said Herbert. "The next rung up the ladder is the instructor. Then assistant professor. Then associate professor. Then full professor. Then dean or president. With each step up, the individual gains in status, salary, tenure. Such is the university ladder to success, heartily endorsed by all and climbed by many."

"That's what I thought too," said the anthropologist gloomily. "Until today."

Herbert waited. He wished he could get over the apprehensive feeling that the primitive masks on the walls were exchanging glances.

"Today," continued the anthropologist, "I met Professor J. Abner Peddiwell, Ph.D., Petaluma College."

"And what did Peddiwell say?"

"This Dr. Peddiwell is an extraordinarily logical man," said the anthropologist, "as readers of his *Saber-Tooth Curriculum* know. So I listened with strict attention to his suggestions for improvements on the ladder to success.

"Dr. Peddiwell said to me, 'Let us take, for example, an eager young man, dewy fresh from graduate courses, inexperienced and anxious to be a staff member of a university. What should be his first post? With his inexperience, it should be a position in which he can do the least possible harm. So his contacts with students and classes should be strictly limited. His opportunities to engage in research and scholarship should be few. He should learn to do many routine, unpleasant chores about the university and thus learn the complexities of the university world.' "

"That sounds sensible," said Herbert. "What is the title of this post for the beginner which Peddiwell so well describes?"

"Dean," said the anthropologist gloomily. "Peddiwell believes that every young staff member should begin as a dean of a college. He believes there is no other post in which a man has fewer contacts with classes and students, fewer opportunities for research and scholarship, more routine, unpleasant chores, and more opportunity to appreciate Allen's universal law."

"I'm afraid I don't follow that last," said Herbert apologetically. "That matter of Allen's Law."

"Peddiwell says that Allen has discovered the only universal law—'things are more complicated than most people think.' "

"But if there aren't enough deanships to go around for all the young men?"

"Make them presidents," said the anthropologist tersely.

"Then after a few years as dean or president—?"

"Promote them to full professorships. Full professors, as you know, usually are men in their later years who work with advanced graduate students in highly theoretical courses. This will be an ideal post for a man in his late twenties, Peddiwell urges. With his own advanced graduate courses only a few years behind him, the young full professor will be an impeccable master of theory which will be unpolluted by practical experience. These young professors will be literally full professors—full of knowledge and panting eagerness to share their own graduate lecture course notes with advanced students. Thus cultural lag will be reduced."

"Then with maturity," surmised Herbert, "the full professor is promoted to an associate professorship. Later the associate professor is promoted to an assistant professorship."

"Right," said the anthropologist. "Finally, as a recognition for distinguished service, the university staff member in his mellow later years may climb to the top rung on the university ladder to success. He will achieve promotion from assistant professor to instructor. All of his matured teaching skills, his ripe knowledge of human beings, his mellow distilled wisdom can be used with large numbers of young undergraduates. He has finally become ready for this most difficult form of teaching. Eventually the old instructor reaches retirement age. Known, heard, beloved by the entire student body, he gracefully withdraws from active service. Then he proceeds to write his doctoral dissertation."

"What!" said Herbert. "Would Peddiwell have him delay his dissertation till after retirement?"

"Yes, indeed," said the anthropologist. "He says that too many dissertations are written before the authors are ready to say anything really significant. They are hurried through so that the young student may receive his union card, a diploma enabling him to teach in the university. How much better, urges Peddiwell, to have the dissertation prepared as the final fruit of a distinguished career. Prepared unhurriedly during long years of retirement that stretch before him; prepared by a seasoned scholar, thoroughly familiar with his sources, library and laboratory. The result: a dissertation respected and read and used by his colleagues, rather than a youthful effort gathering mold in the dusty stacks."

Herbert said, "The mortality rate would cut down on the number of dissertations, too, a distinct gain. But in this series of promotions from dean or president to student, how about salary? How about the tenure granted to full and associate professors and withheld from assistant professors and instructors?"

"Peddiwell has considered that, too," said the anthropologist wearily. "He said to me, 'When does a man most need a president's, a dean's, a full professor's salary? Obviously, when he is a young man in his twenties, furnishing his home, rearing his young children, paying their doctor bills, engaging in a young man's extravagances. When could he afford to live on an instructor's salary, or on a pension while he writes his dissertation? Obviously, in his declining years when worldly desires for material goods are least, when his children have left the nest, when he contentedly looks across the living room at his serene old wife knitting by the fireside. Similarly,' says Peddiwell, 'when does a man most need the protection of tenure laws? During the fiery idealistic days of his youthful fervor or the quiet reflective days of his later years? To ask the question is to answer it.' "

There followed a long silence which Herbert broke.

"Unfortunately, I can see nothing wrong with J. Abner Peddiwell's theory of an improved ladder to success in universities," said Herbert.

"Unfortunately, neither can I," said the anthropologist.

They both sat staring gloomily into the blaze in the great stone fireplace. On the walls, the masks used in primitive ceremonials exchanged winks.

❧ Now I understand why the editor introduced A Fable of Text-book Strategy *as follows, "with no comment whatsoever we present. . . ." An article like this is a sure fire way to lose friends and alienate people. The* Fable *was published in the winter on the eve of the annual February conventions of my trade: the superintendents', the high school principals', the ASCD meetings. I slunk through the meetings, a marked man. Pitifully I protested, "Some of my best friends are textbook writers and publishers." The response was, "Are? Were!"*

10 *A Fable of Textbook Strategy*

As all but the tiniest of you readers know, the world of education has long been divided into warring camps—the traditionalists representing conservatism and the experimentalists representing progressivism. No use blinking the fact—we're Two Worlds and we're locked in grapple. Look at the ways we use materials of instruction, for instance.

Our side—the experimentalists, of course—uses a variety of materials. We use pamphlets and posters, curriculum labs and collected curios, movies and magazines, charts and child creations, film strips and free stuff, best-sellers and biographies, travel and teaching aids, radio and realia, participation and parents. True to our label, we try anything and many things. We're proud of our experimentation, our fertile usages and inventions. Our materials are good for the education of youngsters; they're also of importance in our continuing war against conservatism.

As you know, some of our materials of instruction have proven as attractive as sin or as shiny new toys to some opponents in the enemy's camp. By trying much, and by reporting and sharing our experiences, we have placed many Trojan Horses packed with progressive ideas and approaches within the camp of our enemy, traditionalism. Many traditionalists have been won over.

But still the army of traditionalism is numerically overpowering. We are yet a long way from winning this war for educational democracy. The enemy has a powerful secret weapon!

All captured traditionalists, when disarmed and questioned about their materials of instruction, have reluctantly handed over The Textbook for The Course. Without it, the traditionalist is noticeably nervous and insecure; The Textbook for The Course is apparently a great source of solace and security to him.

It is a strange and wondrous thing—The Textbook for the Course. It is palpable and tangible; it may be held in one's hand and examined. Take, for instance, the recently seized *Atomic Global World and American History*, by the scholarly authors Jukes and Kalikak. It is a singular book.

But The Textbook for The Course is more than singular—it is also plural and multiple. The titles it bears are of infinite variety and it is rumored that its sales are astronomical. Like the nosy, omnipresent Greek gods, The Textbook for The Course is pervasive and may be found everywhere at once. Yet oddly enough, though everywhere, it can exist in splendid isolation.

E Pluribus Unum must be the motto of the enemy camp. For The Textbook for The Course illustrates that out of many comes the one. After the mysteries of textbook selection, The Textbook for The Course regains its singular form in a particular class in a particular school in the army of tradition. Here no competitors appear to dim the glory of The Textbook for The Course, the exclusive fountainhead of truth, the traditionalist's material of instruction and his major weapon.

Struggling against a traditionalism armed with this potent weapon, we experimentalists trouble the heavens with our bootless cries. We deprecate; we deplore; we denounce; we decry. But all too seldom do we try to turn the enemy's major weapon against him. Yet this is the very thing this article proposes as a daring and revolutionary tactic in the great struggle in which we are engaged.

Many will denounce the daring proposal to destroy The Textbook for The Course through adapting it to our purposes. Each of our three popular schools of thought as to textbooks are officially on record against the textbook weapon. The writer hopes he will not be investigated by the Committee on Un-Experimental Activities if he examines each of our schools of thought on the use of textbooks.

Longest established in our camp is "the only good Indian is a dead Indian" group. The name derives from the war cry of our old-time pioneers in experimental education. Let us recall the historic reasoning: textbooks are used by the enemy; the enemy is evil; therefore textbooks are evil. Textbooks are evil; X is a textbook; X is evil. This admirably disposes of the matter save that the textbook does not vanish upon pronouncement of these syllogisms. Even in our own ranks, experimentalists have been discovered surreptitiously using textbooks!

Historically it is not difficult to recognize how "the only good Indian is a dead Indian" school of thought came about. As we all know, the war between traditionalism and experimentalism was begun as a revolution by our liberty-loving ancestors. Our forefathers swung lustily against such inviting targets as authoritarian procedures, divorce from social realities, invalid theory of learning, and the ignoring of needs. The textbook was a neatly-bound-together illustration of the major vices of traditionalism. To it, we experimentalists applied many opprobrious and undoubtedly deserved reproaches. Our milder terms included dull, adult-centered, autocratic, standarized, sterile, and venal.

Many were the stories told at experimentalist campfires of textbook-related barbarisms—the corruption of legislators and educators in the internecine warfare for state adoptions; the craven behavior of authors who doctored and watered down statements, here conveniently forgetting about evolution of which they must have heard tell, there appeasing racist sensibilities in treating of the Civil War or whether Negroes are human beings too, everywhere paying proper respect to Mammon, a potent god.

But not all experimentalists shunned and renounced the textbook in actual fact, though almost all did in public proclamations. Some of our people, as mentioned before, used the device in secret, though they wrote no articles about it. Even more interesting than the hidden addiction of some of our masses, is the "Dr. Jekyll and Mr. Hyde" school of thought which appeared among leaders of our progressive camp, including eminently respectable experimentalists in the best standing.

While he was Dr. Jekyll, the experimentalist would denounce traditionalism and its textbooks with the fervor of an elder of the "Indian" school. At the leading conventions, and with honeyed terms, he would describe the importance of individual differences, of dealing courageously with controversial issues, of presenting alternatives for value application rather than setting forth a fixed truth to be learned, of meeting felt needs, of avoiding sterile question and answer recitations. But in the stillness of night Dr. Jekyll would become Mr. Hyde. And Mr. Hyde would write textbooks. Even his best friends didn't tell him that his textbooks were different from or better than the textbooks of traditionalism, or that they moved conservative users toward more experimental practice. His best friends didn't tell him because of two difficult facts: (a) his texts actually weren't different or better, and (b) as men of the world, his best friends knew why he had really written the textbooks.

Thus the "Jekyll-Hyde" school stood like a colossus with one foot squarely planted in each camp. This might have been a very difficult stance to master had not many of the Jekyll-Hydes been professors of education. As professors they had had long training and experience in inconsistency. To them, dichotomy was normalcy. In many lectures, they condemned lectures. They advocated teacher-pupil planning after they passed out their detailed syllabi on the first day of class. They inveighed against arbitrary assignments and assigned required reading on the matter. Before passing out the A's and F's, they thundered against the tyranny of grades. To college classes of nameless faces they advised knowing the student and meeting his needs. In fact, experience was the creed they advocated daily in the walled-in classroom. The writing of textbooks indistinguishable from those of tradition was obviously only an extension of their professional experiencing. Consequently, textbook writing caused only a few to enter the booby-hatch. Many more paid off their mortgages and lived schizoidly ever after in Paranoid Heights.

Nor does experimentation with the textbook command support among the left wing of experimental education, the "handholders" who form a third school of the matter of textbooks. For the "hand-holders" have denounced the written word itself, along with all ways of learning that fall short of face-to-face contact. In articles and books in which they frequently use strange words, which they apparently coin, they explain that words are useless. Only person-to-person experiences are the real McCoy in changing behavior—experiences like holding cozy conversations. Incidentally, spoken words across a table (which must be round) are regarded as miraculously exempt from the curse of ineffectuality.

The name of this school, "handholders," obviously derives from the theory restrainedly sketched above. "Handholder" carries the three-fold connotation of (1) person-to-person intimacy as the sole road to salvation, (2) holding one's hand from setting pen to paper, and (3) the desirability of hand-to-hand conflict with the enemy who at present unfairly uses many media of public information in a mass-communication world. For the purposes of this investigation it is sufficient to remark that the "handholders" too repudiate the use of the textbook weapon against the enemy, for this is part of their resolute abhorrence of all print—newspapers, magazines, yearbooks, educational periodicals.

So our three prevalent schools of thought are, for varied reasons, unsympathetic to the strategy which is advocated here. Nevertheless, today there are rumblings of dissatisfaction in the ranks of tradition. They must not be ignored—they present an opportunity.

Most of our generals are agreed that the great strategic problem for the experimentalist is how to aid a growing number of dissidents in the ranks of tradition to make their way over to our lines. To this end we establish laboratory schools with functions which might be compared to the decoy duck, did not the analogy seem vaguely unwholesome to this writer. To this end, our men become field consultants and seldom again see their wives and children. To this end, we dangle before the opposition fascinating materials of instruction which sometimes win converts despite qualms about security.

But the potent weapon of the enemy we have renounced. Yet

it is the most powerful material of instruction now in use in schools. If we follow our present policy of denouncing the textbooks and then pretending they aren't there, we shall continue to abdicate as to any real influence. As a result of our abdication, tomorrow's textbooks will continue to be written largely by traditional educators and our Mr. Hydes.

The writer makes bold to suggest that experimentalists experiment with a possible way of moving forward the educational frontier through writing the insights of experimental education into the textbook. Let us destroy The Textbook for The Course through textbooks which will foster teacher-pupil planning, take youth needs as a point of departure, pose situations involving choice among conflicting values, get to grips with vital social realities, encourage wide use of varied materials of instruction.

No experimentalist emancipated from The Textbook for The Course by conversion or grown up in our ranks need protest that he will be forced back into the academic straitjacket. If he has learned to advance democratic purposes and vital education without dependence upon a textbook, more power to him. The new textbook is intended for the many in the camp of tradition who are dissident and unhappy and who might find their way into our ranks if vouchsafed more help. Those who ask for bread will hardly be satisfied with the philosopher's stone. The new textbook is also intended for those in our own ranks who are secretly addicted to The Textbook for The Course. It is for those who are theoretically saved while practically living in sin.

If, for instance, we wish to foster actual teacher-student planning by those who fall into the two broad groups for whom the new material is intended, let us write into the body of our experimental-minded texts illustrations of how teachers and students plan together. Let us so build our texts that further joint planning by teacher and student is essential to complete a process already begun which, in turn, is integral to the structure of the text.

If we wish to foster critical scrutiny of conflicting value patterns and consequently to help students to reconstruct their experiences, let us create situations in texts in which values conflict and students must choose. For instance, instead of blatantly or tacitly expounding any one approach to economic thought, we might consider the pros and cons not only of conflicting economic interpretations but also of the basic assumptions which underlie each interpretation—particularly the philosophical, psychological, and historical assumptions. We can construct texts which, instead of presenting a witches' brew of uninterpreted facts, pave the way for intelligent discussion of value issues.

If we wish to encourage broad use of varied materials of instruction, let us be fertile in our suggestions. Has anyone ever used a battery of materials and a meaningful approach through the pedestrian lists of suggested activities tacked on the ends of chapters? We need no bustles on the rears of our chapters. We'll get maximal use of a variety of materials on the part of our users if we disperse throughout the text a range of things to do which are exactly right for the occasion. When recommending movies related to a topic, our experimentalist will not be content with a vague benign endorsement; he'll both refer to the film catalogue and give book, chapter, and verse on specific available movies. When writing of possible community participation activities. he'll mention specific past precedents as well as dream up recommendations.

Always the writer will present several possibilities, multiple media, the varied ways of learning. Always the effort will be to help the teacher to be free. Emancipation alone is not enough; in education we have found that many, free in theory, have in reality clung fondly to their chains.

Great will be the head shaking in the councils of the experimentalists at this proposal for destroying The Textbook for The Course by turning against the enemy experimental models of his ancient blunderbuss. "The only good Indian is a dead Indian" school will stalwartly, though a bit repetitiously, advance the contention that the only good Indian is a dead Indian. The "hand-holders" will shake their heads pityingly and will continue calling for hand-to-hand struggles in this age of mass communication. Worst of all, the "Dr. Jekyll and Mr. Hyde" school will first wait to see whether the proposal gains acceptance and, if it does, claim that this is just what they have been doing all along.

Thus the difference between the Jekyll-Hydes and the few venturesome souls who have been actually attempting the strategy here recommended may become as blurry as a reactionary newspaper's distinctions as to communists and liberals. To differentiate among the two schools, fortunately we can still use the Biblical injunction, "By their works shall ye know them."

It will be argued that the weapon-makers, the publishers, may get wind of the real purpose of the Machiavellian scheme, the destruction of The Textbook for The Course—and with it the enemy, traditionalism. If so, it will be said, the publishers may be shrewd enough to refuse to publish our books. This, however, seems an unlikely move on the part of the makers of weapons, the merchants of death who publish The Textbook. If what these merchants refer to as a "demand" develops, they will go along with one eye on trends, one on sales, and with both hands clutching a financial statement. Despite the briskness of business at present, the brighter among them indicate a worried willingness to move in the experimental direction if they can find out what in thunder it is.

Basically, however, fear of the merchants of death getting wind of the scheme and related fear that traditionalists will stiffen their resistance if their counter-propaganda tips them off are equally groundless. The secret of our daring proposal is safe since no traditionalist and no conservative publisher reads a publication such as this. For if they did, how could they remain traditional or educationally conservative?

The column on John Dewey's Disciples made the impact of a rose leaf falling into the Grand Canyon. I'm sure it was published; I even have the issue. But I never found anyone who has read it. Maybe it struck too close to home. Maybe it hit a sensitive nerve among my colleagues.

I think the modern educator should make clear to himself and the public his independence of father figures. Too often these days he is being attributed a doctrinaire orthodoxy, a frozen attitude toward educational ideas, which should be no part of his equipment in a dynamic age of swift educational and social change. Therefore this lightly phrased yet seriously intended declaration of educational independence.

11 *John Dewey's Disciples*

It was one of those rare mornings when they could linger over coffee. The night before he had met with the curriculum committee and also had addressed the junior high school PTA. At the PTA he had valiantly explained the common learnings course to assorted upper-middle class matrons obsessed with little Willie's college entrance requirements. This morning was a time of deserved armistice.

Over the coffee cups and the peaceful rustle of the morning newspaper, his wife said, "I see by the papers that there were big doings in celebration of John Dewey's ninetieth birthday. Editorials on the grand old man of modern education, dinners at $7.50 a plate, a special issue of the *New Republic*, meetings and papers in universities across the nation. Here's an educator who says that Dewey is forever enshrined, for his writings are the fount of all educational knowledge. He goes on to say that Dewey has pronounced the ultimate word in world thought."

"To think that it's happening to John Dewey too," he said.

"John Dewey of all people. Confucius, Aristotle, the Christian saints, Plato, Marx, Gandhi. And now John Dewey. A murrain upon his disciples!"

"And what on earth is wrong with being a disciple of John Dewey?"

"Menace to experimental education," he said briefly.

"Look, darling," she said. "You're a curriculum director. You've spent your life putting John Dewey's ideas into practice in public schools. You're a disciple of John Dewey yourself!"

"Not guilty, Judge."

"The number of pork chops and frilly little dresses I've sacrificed while you pursued advanced degrees and the understanding of John Dewey! The quotes housing unquotes I've lived in during the process! The good things you've always said about John Dewey in your talks and in your graduate papers! And now you tell me that John Dewey's admirers are a menace because they give him birthday parties. *Now* you tell me!"

"Not John Dewey's admirers, dear," he said, "and nothing to do with his birthday celebrations either. For that matter, nothing to do with societies that carry forward his work or with the many creative educators who study and use and extend Dewey's insights. I said *disciples*. Is there any more coffee?"

"This," she mused aloud, "is probably one of those cases of self-hate I've read about. Or maybe it's the death wish. Shall I make you an appointment with a psychiatrist, dear?"

"Ever hear what Sam Goldwyn is supposed to have said about people who go to psychiatrists?" he asked, returning from the kitchen with the coffee pot. "Anybody who goes to a psychiatrist should have his head examined."

"Or maybe," she pursued, "at the PTA last night you were converted by those matrons out of the Helen Hokinson drawings in the *New Yorker*. So now our school system will advance briskly backward to the classics. Mental discipline and college entrance requirements *uber alles*. I'll have to brush up on the hundred great books."

"I think I'll heat up this coffee," he said. "Cold."

"I can wait," said his wife. "Schoolmen's wives are a patient lot. I can wait."

"It's like this," he said from the kitchen. "By disciple I mean the person who treats Dewey's writings as though they were the final authority, the truth with a capital T, the eternal verity. A Dewey disciple—not a Dewey student or admirer, mind you— seems to regard Dewey's writings as a body of sacred writ. He quarrels with other disciples over the 'true' meaning of the writ. To 'prove' pet contentions, he cites something Dewey wrote near the turn of the nineteenth century. His opponent, in turn, proves the contrary by quoting something Dewey wrote forty years later. Each regards deviation from Dewey as the ultimate in heresy—unless the master can be cited to justify the deviation. They sound like two comrades confounding each other with quotations from Marx and Lenin on the correct interpretation of the current party line. Unconsciously these disciples are authoritarian, not experimental. Regarding Dewey's great contribution as a gospel denies everything Dewey stands for! That's not what old John means at all!"

"Care to quote from his writings to prove that?" she inquired delicately. Properly, he paid no heed.

He summarized. "There's a great difference between the students of Dewey and the disciples of Dewey. Disciples turn Dewey's magnificent contribution into authoritarian dogma, complete with writ, expounders, and disputatious sects. They turn Dewey into a saint." He chuckled. "I suppose he's the first relativistic saint in all history."

As she poured their last cups of hot coffee, his wife said, "Maybe we should leave confusing things like these to philosophers, dear."

IV
Meeting Forces
Affecting
Education

The Background

It is characteristic of our times that the modern educator with a conscience must give some of his time to meeting reactionary forces which would censor the free use of intelligence in the public schools. Invalid viewpoints should not pass unanswered, whispers the Puritan heritage. Pressure groups should not indoctrinate and impose their peculiar notions on free men's schools. So I'll have my say; I'll answer the misinterpreters; I'll defend an education for democracy.

From this decision forward, the way is paved with traps. Despite the irresponsibility of many critics, the modern educator must not respond in kind—which means that since conflict and dramatic overstatement made news, the respondent doesn't achieve the headlines or the air waves. He must not become defensive or even lay himself open to the suspicion of defensiveness —for defense wins no wars. He must resist the temptation to proclaim that the schools are doing beautifully—for well does he know they are not.

The heyday of the attacks on the public schools by reactionary forces came as the nineteen forties became the fifties. Some outstanding superintendents, like Willard Goslin of Pasadena, were forced to resign. Proposals for textbook censorship were rife. Right wing organizations labelled individual educators and educational associations as subversive. Guilt by association was rampant.

The attacks by reactionaries on the public schools coincided with the phenomenon called McCarthyism. It is little wonder that it did, for the reactionary assault on public schools was the educational counterpart of McCarthyism.

To be an egghead in the late forties and early fifties was to be out of fashion, not *de rigueur* as today. To be an educator with ideas about social education in the early fifties was to be suspect automatically. To act on those ideas was to make one a target for mud and vitriol. They were strange days for educators, who are largely gentle people.

I recall how hard it was for me to decide that I had to fight an extremist censorship bill introduced in the Illinois Legislature. I would have preferred to "let George do it." But I had to be one of the Georges by virtue of being the professor of social studies education in the University of Illinois. The bill was killed in committee; I learned that despite the mass appearance of political organizations, a few individuals can make a very large difference.

Our national insanity, along with its educational counterpart, is past. May its grave be deep and its revival abortive! And may the proponents of democratic education for free men recognize that the George of "let George do it" can only be ourselves, eternally vigilant.

And, incidentally, may the proponents of democratic education recognize a clear-cut difference between the reactionary forces and the academic critics of modern education who are frequently heard today. The latter group are men of good will who happen to see education differently from some others of us, as the last entry in this section attempts to show.

⳺§ The Climate of Fear *was inspired by the fanatical vigilantes of the McCarthy era who tried to censor and coerce American education. Admittedly there was more than a touch of anger in the satire. Dim-witted reactionaries wrapped in the flag and boasting of 100 per cent Americanism had adopted the totalitarian techniques of equally dim-witted communists. Perhaps it was the underlying serious message of the column which led some readers, to my amazement and horror, to take my words soberly. A few told me in dead earnest of far rightists whom they suspected to be actually representatives of the Communist Party. Maybe, in these complex times, aspiring satirists will have to label their output "take with several grains of salt." As Professor Americus' colleague said, "You can't be too careful, you know."*

12 *The Climate of Fear*

PASSING Professor Americus' abandoned desk, his colleague noticed some sheets protruding from a pigeonhole. Hoping he was unobserved, he pulled out Professor Americus' last manuscript and began to read:

"I don't know exactly when the horrid suspicion first came to me that the Communist Party in America, rebuffed by left-of-center organizations, had successfully infiltrated highly conservative right-wing organizations. Intent newspaper reading has now convinced me that there could be no other reasonable explanation of what was happening. Unsuccessful in their energetic bid to dominate the American left, the Communists apparently had changed the party line again. Communists and their fellow travelers were now instructed to take over the key positions in the most respectable, patriotic, 100% conservative groups. They had developed a diabolic new tactic and they were rapidly gaining control of patriotic societies, the right-wing press, and anti-subversive committees of Congress and the state legislatures!

"I must confess that, up until the time of my horrid realization, I had always considered American Communists to be singularly dim-witted and ludicrous dunderheads. With each reversal of party strategy, they skidded like burlesque comedians. Each new inanity was cloaked in pretentious, pseudo-scientific jargon. Their fronts were as transparent as Macy's display windows; a moderately intelligent seven-year-old could see through them. To put it in American folk language, to me the Communists just didn't seem real bright.

"Until late in the nineteen-forties, it appeared that in America their curious religion would remain the exclusive property of their small disputatious sect. They fought a losing battle in the CIO; their intellectuals jumped off the train at particularly tortuous turnings of the party line; their shenanigans with parliamentary rules were fathomed and overcome; their endorsement was the kiss of death for national political candidates. Direct attempts to teach Americans to accept communist principles and techniques were farcical failures save in a few isolated precincts of New York City. But then—alas!—some unknown, sinister, brilliant comrade developed the fiendishly simple tactic that is now working.

"The diabolic tactic was to teach Americans to adopt communistic principles and approaches in fighting communism. While apparently combating Communists in this country, Americans would learn to accept communist techniques. For instance, basic to communist policies and practices and repugnant to democracy are suppression of minority political parties when there is no clear and present danger, accusations of disloyalty without adequate opportunity for defense, past as well as present political orthodoxy as a condition of all employment, creation of confusion as to who really believes what. So, naturally, a first step in the diabolic new tactic was to apply these communist ways to American conditions in an attempt to create the climate of fear so characteristic of the communist state. When democratic-minded men protested these communist methods, they could be accused of communist sympathies, discredited, and removed from responsible positions. Eventually all loyalty to democratic principles and methods would be suspected as communistic. An unconsciously communistic America could readily shift to conscious communism through Communists in key positions in the conservative anti-communist crusade.

"I know it seems completely fantastic and unthinkable to believe that the Communists are disguising themselves as conservatives in groups that have always asserted the highest patriotism, Americanism, loyalty, and anti-communism. I know it is completely incredible to believe that communistic conservatives are spreading communist principles and techniques in the name of anti-communism in order to establish communism here! But how else can we explain recent proposals?

"Censorship of textbooks is advocated so that our boys and girls will not learn about countries wicked and stupid enough to censor textbooks. Is this not a trick to establish the Soviet doctrine that textbooks should be censored?

"We are urged to ban and bar and drop from reading lists and libraries a variety of publications, ranging from non-communist liberal materials to the tedious classics of the Marxist ideology, in order to protect ourselves from a police state education that bans and bars and drops from reading lists and libraries a variety of publications. Is this not a sly trick to establish the Soviet doctrine of contempt for the method of intelligence?

"Legislative enforcement in one great American state contemplates having teachers 'report' on organizations and activities of colleagues while others report on the reporters. This is advocated to defend us from ever living in a spy state like the Soviet Union where teachers report others for suspected heresies. Another trick?

"Pressure groups caution administrators and teachers against full and free discussion of certain controversial issues for the pressure groups fear such discussion will lead to that undemocratic day when controversial issues will not be freely and fully discussed.

"What American would propose such policies and methods as these save Communists, fellow travelers, or their innocent dupes?

The guilt by association of the sponsors of these and many other allied steps seems inescapable.

"The result is the spread of the climate of fear. As in the totalitarian state, educators think to themselves. 'You can't be too careful, you know'. . . ."

Here the manuscript of Professor Americus broke off suddenly, unfinished. Apparently he was in the midst of writing when he was brought up before the board of trustees on charges of subversive activities. Testimony brought out the facts that he had a foreign-sounding name, that he had once spoken critically of a member of the United States Senate (Huey P. Long), and that his wife occasionally dined with a woman whose sister was said to have contributed to an ambulance fund for the Spanish Loyalists. Currently Professor Americus is too busy to write further as he attempts, so far without success, to find a post following his dismissal.

His colleague looked about, frowned, and carefully tore Professor Americus' last manuscript into a thousand pieces. If someone had been watching, his own attitude toward the eccentric and unreliable Professor Americus was thus made unmistakably clear. Thought Professor Americus' colleague—*you can't be too careful, you know.*

Educational Freedom in an Age of Anxiety *was the John Dewey Society's response to the cultural vigilantes who attempted to bully educators in the early nineteen fifties. My introduction to the volume was an impressionistic attempt to place the current conflict over freedom in its proper historical setting.*

13 *Educational Freedom in an Age of Anxiety*

THE ISSUES are clear:

The issue of freedom of inquiry versus inculcation of fixed answers.

The issue of the right of individuals to decide from among possibilities versus imposition on people of somebody's pet truth.

The issue of freedom of education versus censorship of education.

The issue, essentially, of the democratic method of intelligence versus the authoritarian method of "telling them."

These are old issues. They have been and will be the cause of many struggles in the history of ideas. Man's fight for freedom has taken place on strange battlefields.

A court in Athens where a citizen was on trial charged with "corrupting the young."

A room where an Englishman, who was yet to write *Paradise Lost*, wrote in his pamphlet defending freedom of the press, "He who destroys a good book kills reason itself."

A Rhode Island wilderness through which trudged a refugee from Puritans who had come to the New World to worship God as they saw fit—and to force others to do the same.

Nineteenth-century England, where a libertarian, John Stuart Mill, put aside political economy to write *On Liberty*, "It is not the mind of heretics that are deteriorated most by the ban placed on all inquiry which does not end in the orthodox conclusions. The greatest harm done is to those who are not heretics, and whose whole mental development is cramped, and their reason cowed, by fear of heresy."

An American presidential inauguration when the great architect of the Declaration of Independence said, "Error of opinion may be tolerated where reason is left free to combat it."

An American presidential inauguration in 1933, when a resonant voice said confidently, "The only thing we have to fear is fear itself."

The chambers of the Supreme Court, where a Yankee from Olympus spoke out:

"But when men have realized that time has upset many fighting faiths, they may come to believe even more than they believe the very foundation of their own conduct that the ultimate good desired is better reached by free trade in ideas— that the best test of truth is the power of thought to get itself accepted in the competition of the market, and that truth is the only ground on which their wishes can be carried out. That at any rate is the theory of our Constitution."

Still today the old issues are at the heart of man's struggles. The conflicts over educational freedom in the 1950's still take place on strange battlegrounds:

The crowded committee room in a Midwest state capitol where undramatic people wait patiently to appear before a committee in opposition to a proposed textbook censorship bill.

The editorial offices of a great South American daily which presumed to speak against the regime of dictator Peron.

The board room of a great American state university where board members are deciding whether or not to subvert the principles of free inquiry on which the university was founded.

The office of a puppet commissar in Czechoslovakia where communist inquisitors question a sleepless teacher until he invents a confession.

The office of a university professor where he searches his files and writings at midnight for evidence to prove what to the searcher had always seemed obvious, his loyalty; he has received an unexpected call to appear before a committee investigating un-American activities.

The strangest battlefield of all is man's mind.

A teacher in Portland (whether Maine or Oregon makes no difference) cynically wondering what topics are "too hot" this year for consideration in social studies by youngsters old enough to fight in wars.

A teacher in Springfield (whether Massachusetts, Illinois, Ohio, or Vermont doesn't matter) deciding whether to use an established standard textbook attacked as radical in Texas.

A teacher in Metropolis (whether New York, Chicago, Los Angeles, or Philadelphia doesn't matter) trying to decide whether joining World Federalists would peril her job.

A teacher in American City, USA, fearing freedom, fleeing from liberty, and gratefully returning to the security of the formal recitation.

Another teacher in American City, USA, thumbtacking on the faculty bulletin board an NEA poster, "Free men cannot be taught properly by slaves. Courageous citizens cannot be well educated by scared hired men."

An editor in the South wondering how much space he should give a dramatic, yet patently irresponsible, attack on the local schools.

A bright young Middle-Western college graduate wondering whether to rule out government employment as a career because "they call you a security risk if you have any ideas different from Grover Cleveland."

A clergyman in New England thinking about his position on released time for religious instruction.

A businessman in the Rocky Mountain states wondering whether he should join a local committee on schools.

A patrioteer-for-pay on the West Coast thumbing through his file and deciding on the next target.

A school administrator in the Southwest trying to decide what questions he might ethically ask an applicant for a job.

An East Coast communist grinning over a reactionary newspaper's smear of an anti-communist as communist.

Freedom of inquiry is what distinguishes us from the totalitarians.

*⫷§ The criticism of modern schools by academic critics is a very
different thing from the political onslaughts of the reactionary forces.
Yet some school people are in danger of confusing the two and blur-
ring the very real distinction between them. The vituperation which
both reactionary forces and academic critics substitute on occasion
for evidence and logic encourages obfuscation.*

*My talk to the National Society of College Teachers of Education
was an attempt to define the differences and examine the types of
criticisms while extending a hand in cooperation. Whether one can
simultaneously twit the academic critics yet offer a path toward re-
conciliation is, I must admit in retrospect, at least debatable. Below
are my comments which I addressed to my colleagues, the teachers
of teachers.*

14 *Attitudes Toward Teacher Education*

"LAY ATTITUDES TOWARD TEACHER EDUCATION." As a speaker, I
took the liberty of dropping the word "lay" when I discovered
that not many lay people have discernible attitudes toward the
education of teachers. This I learned through a scholarly technique made famous by one of the academic critics of teacher education. You may recall that a botany professor asked a hundred
and six people, whom he met over a ten-year period in such
places as trains and barber shops and hotel lobbies, whether the
schools were going to the dogs. The magazine of the American
Association for the Advancement of Science, in which his article appeared, solemnly reproduced a page-wide table of his findings.

Encouraged by the ease of such scholarship, I asked everybody
I met on the train en route from Nashville to Chicago about
their lay attitudes toward teacher education. I found that most
of them didn't have any. To insure a scientific sampling of all

social classes, I even included smokers in the washrooms of *both* pullmans and day coaches.

The absence of attitudes on the part of my respondents reminded me of one of the Boyd H. Bode legends. Bode once opened his class in philosophy of education at Ohio State University by telling the students that he had a new definition of philosophy. As the students paused, with pencils quivering to await the new revelation, Bode said that he had overheard a conversation between two women. One was consoling the other whose husband had just joined the late dear departed. She advised the bereaved widow, "Dear, just be philosophical about it. Don't think about it at all." In the same way, most people seem to be philosophical about teacher education.

On the other hand, we college teachers of education are not philosophical about teacher education. We think about it all the time. We live with it day and night. Our constant effort is to improve it.

We in teacher education are peculiarly sensitive to currents of opinion in our professional field. We are especially sensitive to criticisms. That the critics may be few in number, doesn't particularly comfort us. History has often been made by minorities.

Who are our major critics? Some educators would include one or more philanthropic organizations with the magical word "fund" in their titles. But the granters of subsidies assure us that they engage in "experiments," not criticisms. Oddly enough, this interpretation seems to be accepted more often by college administrators seeking grants than by lowly professors of education.

Since the jury has not yet brought in a clear verdict on what Edwin R. Embree called the philanthropoids, let us consider instead two acknowledgedly critical camps: the reactionary forces and the academic critics.

The reactionary forces are made up of extreme right wing organizations which attempt to force on the schools their peculiar notions of economic and political reaction and ultra-nationalistic patrioteering. They attack the schools as communistic because school men, believers in the free play of intelligence, will not join in their reactionary crusade to repeal the twentieth century. Typically, the organizations of the reactionary forces oppose such reforms as the income tax, the Tennessee Valley Authority, and social security. They oppose international organizations such as the UN and most particularly UNESCO. As part of their campaign, they also oppose adequate support for public education. At their mildest, they are tax-cutters with respect to public education. At their wildest, they betray their intentions in pamphlets with lurid titles. Harold Benjamin accurately characterized this group as early as 1947 when he called them "enemies of public education."

Teacher education is just one of the targets of the enemies of the public schools. We in teacher education happen to come under fire because we are articulate. We do write articles, edit magazines, and develop many ideas which are tried out in the laboratories of teachers' colleges and public school systems. The reactionary forces, themselves unabashed indoctrinators of far right-wing ideologies, attack us as indoctrinating leftists. They apparently share Knute Rockne's theory that the best defense is a good offense. The psychologists call it projection.

The reactionary forces illustrate the power of cultural lag in that only recently have they discovered the nineteen thirties. Invariably, their tirades against American teacher education are ornamented by selected quotations from the social reconstructionists of the nineteen thirties. Their favorite texts are taken from the spiritual and emotional despair of the great depression. Individuals are cited and grossly distorted. An occasional excess is regarded as the rule. Then there is a leap to the generalization that the excess or the grossly distorted citation of an individual's opinion represents all of education now.

But today this particular brand of attack on American education seems to have been turned back. The mild-mannered educators did not prove so easy a target after all. Many of them fought back on the national level through articles and pamphlets and books. They gave time that they would rather have invested in scholarship to the unrewarding chore of meeting the attacks. The authors of books like *Educational Freedom in An Age of Anxiety, Freedom in Public Education, Forces Affecting American Education* and many others were engaged in a necessary defensive action. They never satisfied some of the militants in the profession who apparently wanted them to attack any individual or organization or church that disagreed with the individual militant's personal philosophy of education. From the letters they received, it sometimes seemed to the defenders of education that only the reactionaries read the books.

Nineteen forty-nine to nineteen fifty-three were the high years of the reactionary attack upon education, including teacher education. In community after community, local men and women of good will built coalitions and fought their unheralded, unsung, local defenses. Today, I often hear of the debt of gratitude which education owes to the men who organized the National Citizens Commission for the Public Schools. I certainly agree. But if I had to single out one sex for credit, I would single out the gallant women of organizations like the American Association of University Women, the League of Women Voters, and the PTA who fought and won skirmish after skirmish on the local level.

In this struggle between St. George and the dragon—and naturally I am casting teacher educators in the role of St. George—there was no clean-cut victory, no telling final thrust with the lance. Instead, the dragon was clumsily but gallantly clobbered by St. George. Somehow the dragon eventually pooped out.

Only time will tell whether the dragon fell into a temporary or a permanent decease. At least the times are somewhat safer than they were. Even the lofty now are coming out of their ivory towers to tell those who fought in the campaign that it really wasn't necessary and that dragons die of their own weight. Someone should interview the dragon sometime on this question.

A second criticism leveled at teacher education comes from a currently more vigorous and influential group. Archibald Anderson, the editor of *Educational Theory*, first popularized the term academic critic. The most persistent academic critic is a professor of history. Another is a professor of botany, another a professor of chemistry, another an advertising man, another a former college president, another a journalist, and so forth. They have their disciples who write follow-up articles and a flock of faithful, number unknown, who write letters to the editor and distribute reprints. Though candor compels us to recognize that liberal arts professors are prominent among the academic critics, let us not erroneously believe that a majority of academic scholars share the excessive viewpoints of the academic critics.

The academic critics do resemble St. George more than they resemble the dragon. They certainly are not enemies of public education. (Incidentally, in article after article, they lose no opportunity to remind us of this. In martyred tones, they write, "I know I will be called an enemy of education for writing this but . . ."). They are not economic, political, ultra-nationalistic reactionaries. (Some of them remind us of this by their conscious choice of publication outlets, including the *New Republic*, the *Reporter*, and the *Atlantic Monthly*.) They are not even tax-cutters; they join us in whooping it up for more money for the schools. They believe in our republican form of government. They are fond of America too. They do happen to disagree with many professors of education on how best to educate Americans.

The academic critics can best be met through the free trade in ideas of which Justice Holmes wrote. Teacher educators must do more than rebut. Teachers of education must set forth their own ideas not only for the profession but in books for the citizen and in articles or popular magazines. They must communicate their versions of education for a democracy.

There is no better way of playing into the hands of the academic critics than suggesting to editors that the critics shouldn't be published. In response, the academic critics scream bloody murder and academic freedom and "we told you it was a conspiracy." So, quoting Voltaire and feeling like the American Civil Liberties Union defending Gerald L. K. Smith's right to free speech, teacher educators must then come to the defense of free expression by critics.

What are the academic critics saying about teacher education? Nothing very new, the usual ancient false charges. They charge that teacher education scorns the scholarship and contributions of the liberalizing content of the curriculum. They argue that teacher education has multiplied the courses in education which the prospective teacher or teacher in service must take and thus has drowned out all else. They charge that teacher education has gained control of the apparatus of public education and manipulates it. They disapprove of elementary and secondary schools in which youngsters come to grips with problems, based on needs and social realities and reflective thinking. All of this, they say, adds up to a contribution by teacher education to the decline of the education of youth in America. The target of the academic critics is not education in general; it is specifically the college teachers of education who are cast in the villain's role.

One sometimes suspects that the anger aroused in teacher educators comes as much from the choice of language by some of the recent academic critics as from the charges. Some of the academic critics have gaudy vocabularies, a gift of irony, and a flair for billingsgate. It is difficult for a teacher educator to keep his mind on the argument as he reads of "dreary intellectual sinks and their often dismal practitioners," of "otiose emphasis on the obvious," and "a frequent dissemination of false notions," or whatever is your own favorite quotation. When such luxuriant language is coupled with dependence on third-hand sources, interviews in barber shops, quotations out of context, lack of carry-over of research methodology from an academic discipline to the area of education, the enraged teacher educator is tempted to reply in kind. Some of the professors of education are competent word-slingers and satirists themselves.

Perhaps intercultural or intergroup education must now be expanded to include not only relationships among races, religions, nationalities, and social classes, but also relationships among professors. The parallels are as obvious as they are ludicrous. Maybe the professors of education are to take the place of Jews in the new demonology. The old racist demonology stereotyped all Jews as conspiratorial, clannish, and wicked. In the new demonology, all this applies to the teacher educators. In the old demonology, the Jews were also grasping, covetous and tricky. So it is supposed to be with the Machiavellian teacher educators. The analogy breaks down at one point; no racist ever accused the Jews of being stupid and plain ignorant.

The old and the new demonologies readily attribute polar opposite characteristics to the demons. For instance, the Jews were held simultaneously to be clannish and constantly pushing in where they weren't wanted. They were held to be simultaneously capitalistic and communist. Similarly the new demonology holds that the teacher educator is abysmally ignorant, yet wise as the serpent in rigging the system. The teacher educator is supposed to believe that schools should teach no content and at the same time believe that schools should teach the wrong content. The teacher educator is supposed to teach only a mess of methods courses and simultaneously spend all of his time in the basement of education teaching foundations. The teacher educator is supposed to oppose the use of the intellect by young people and simultaneously to greatly overemphasize problem-solving.

To carry the intercultural analogy a step further, we might consider what good intercultural education theory would say about handling human relations problems among professors. The most obvious first recommendation would be to avoid counterstereotyping. Let us not develop in teacher education our own version of demonology. With the semanticists, professors of education should perhaps murmur each night on going to bed, "Liberal arts professor A is not liberal arts professor B." The academic critics are a small minority, however articulate, among liberal arts professors.

But, more positively, teacher educators might take a cue from human relations education and build bridges of good will. As any human relations consultant can tell us, this involves working together for common purposes, finding common ground, communicating, communicating, communicating. Teacher education scholars and academic scholars have many common problems: good teaching, sound scholarship, more teachers, more buildings, better salaries, the elimination of ignorance, the creation of a better society, the development of supporting sciences based on solid research.

The results in the general community of scholars to which liberal arts and teacher educators belong might be remarkable. Given enough time, an academic scholar and a professional education scholar might come to understand the common elements in one's emphasis on intellectual training and the other's emphasis on the method of intelligence. Those who are proud of teaching subject matter and those who are proud of teaching people might come to see that people have to do the learning of significant subject matter. Those who work in the academic disciplines and those who work in the professional courses might even come to see that in the making of a good teacher it is necessary to keep more than one thing in mind at the same time!

Who knows where a quest conducted reasonably and with emphasis on common concepts might take us?

V

*Working for
Better Relations
Among Groups*

The Background

I SUSPECT that I first became an advocate of education for better relationships among Americans of varied races, religions, and nationality backgrounds when I was a high school student and my "bunch" was made up of Joey Carter, Sidney Goldberg, Randy Hansen, and Bobby Crockard, who were, respectively, of Negro, Jewish, Swedish, and Scotch backgrounds. Such are the divergences of occupational and educational paths in Megalopolis that we never saw each other again after a few post-high school years. But while we were in high school we taught each other mutual acceptance and never knew we were doing so.

As a liberal of the depression years I held to racial equality in the characteristic orthodox and almost unreflective way of many liberals. I never thought much about the intricacies of building better relationships among groups until it became my professional responsibility as publications director for the Bureau for Intercultural Education. Even then the problem was academic; I developed educational techniques and embodied them in writings.

While I taught at the University of Illinois, my appointment to the Governor's Illinois Interracial Commission nudged me out of the ivory tower and on to the field of battle. Problems of intergroup relations become more real when you meet the problem of a concessionaire at the reproduction of Abraham Lincoln's village, New Salem, turning away Negro students from the restaurant; a Negro shopper finding that she can try on hats but not coats in a store in a local community (across the street she can try on coats but not hats); a Negro movie goer being thumbed to the balcony in one theater, turned away at another, admitted freely to a third, and seated at a fourth only if accompanied by a small white child. I began to see that you need a guide to conflicting patterns of segregation if you are a Northern Negro. Either that or community action to supplement education.

Yet community action posed many problems. The phone rang one spring day in 1949. Governor Adlai E. Stevenson's secretary was on the wire. A few hours later I was in the southern Illinois community of Alton to play a new role, that of mediator. In one of America's earliest racial "sit-ins," the Negro population sent its small children day after day to sit in the rooms and corridors of the all-white elementary schools nearest the homes of the Negro children. Threatening knots of whites clustered outside the buildings. Any "incident" could be the fuse of an explosion.

The school board and administration wouldn't give nor would the Negro population. The twain wouldn't even confer, so I shuttled between them with proposals. With proof established that school segregation was a fact, hundreds of members of the Negro community gathered in a church one night, with one white person present, the mediator, and voted to call off the sit-in and to bring their case to the courts. I got my first sleep in forty-eight hours. When tense Alton woke next morning and photographers and groups of whites gathered outside the schools not a Negro child appeared. The crisis was over. After legal proceedings were initiated, the board desegregated the elementary schools.

When George Peabody College for Teachers in 1951 invited me South to teach and head a division of the college in Nashville, Tennessee, my major hesitancy was whether a Yankee with my convictions could be effective in community life in the South. The advice of an old friend, Charles S. Johnson, the late president of Fisk University and a Negro, was that some Yankees could, that it depended on how a person operated. So my work brought me South to watch the impact of the Supreme Court decision against segregation in 1954 and to play some part as Nashville was forced to face the reality of school integration.

For me, education for better relationships among groups combines several strands that I find essential if I am to feel that what I'm doing adds up and makes some difference, however small, in the world. Education for democratic human relations is an authentic contemporary expression of liberalism and social reform. It is a vehicle for curriculum change toward modern problem-centered education. It is a challenge to anybody's capacity for scholarship and leadership. I plan to keep working away on our American problems of group relationships whatever my assignment as an educator or my locale.

◆§ Nothing is more practical than theory. Nothing is sadder than dedication of one's life to practice based on invalid theory. We ignore theory at mortal peril to the meaningfulness of our work in education.

So I tell my teacher education students. Most of them continue to look skeptical. They hunger after a goddess called "the practical", a bitch goddess devoid of theoretical parentage.

To attempt to take the curse off theory, I have tried on occasion to popularize some abstract ideas on education even to introducing characters as a vehicle for carrying my convictions on the foundations of the curriculum. In this book you won't catch me saying baldly, as I did in my doctoral dissertation entitled A Social Living Curriculum for Postwar Secondary Education: An Approach to Curriculum Development Through Centers of Experience Based on the Interaction of Values, Social Realities, and Needs *(had enough?): "This dissertation recommends an approach to curricula in social living for postwar secondary education. The approach holds that three sources are in interaction: values, social realities, and needs of adolescents. Desirable curricula are derived from these sources. Fifteen centers of experience are recommended. Each is based upon values, social realities, and needs of adolescents—the three curricular sources which interact."*

But that's what I mean. That's also what the workshop staff member means when he applies the theory to education for better group relations in the excerpt from the yearbook Intercultural Attitudes in the Making *which follows.*

15 *Intercultural Attitudes in the Making*

THE teachers in service who made up Middletown's Curriculum Workshop were considering a panel report. The topic was: "What Curricular Experiences Are Essential in a High School Program?" Ann Smith rated it one of the best sessions she had attended during the summer weeks. She kept wishing that more of her colleagues from West High were registered in the workshop. At the moment, the panel members were discussing experiences in intercultural education as among the essentials in today's school program. Ann listened intently; the field of human relations was the area on which she was concentrating in the workshop.

One teacher was urging, "If the members of this workshop intend to stress the most needed centers of experience in the program of today's high school, they must include intercultural education. In my school, cliques dominate some clubs; kids of lower-class background and of foreign parentage do not even try to join these clubs any more. Jewish youngsters cannot gain full acceptance; the invisible walls rise at school social affairs, for instance. We have had our share of locker room and corridor 'incidents' between Negroes and whites. Nasty names get tossed about lightly, whether in the balcony chatter at basketball games or in would-be humor over the cokes.

"But if you ask the faculty or administration about tensions, you get that big bland smile and the classic response, 'We have no problems here.' I would certainly rank intercultural education high among essential experiences because of the outstanding importance of problems of human relations in the lives of many students I meet."

"The conflicts you mention are not obvious with us," added another panel participant. "The youngsters who come to our high school are largely white, native-born, and Protestant. Yet I, too, would urge intercultural education as an essential in the modern American high school, regardless of what has to be shoved aside to make room for it. But I have another reason— the brutal facts of life in the society these kids are inheriting. These youngsters are going to live in a society in which prejudice, discrimination, and bigotry are wicked realities. It is a world still all too familiar with racism, anti-Semitism, lonely refugees. You do not have to look far from home to recognize that the war against fascism is not over even in our own country.

"As a matter of fact, you do not have to look any farther than our own community. Our community has slum housing for Negroes and restrictive covenants to 'keep them in their place.' It has 'Christians only' advertising, and snobbish clubs, and queries about nationality and religion on employment blanks, and newspaper editorials against the admission of refugees to a land where Liberty is getting weary of holding up her torch."

A third panel member chipped in: "But there is an even sounder reason for dealing with racial, religious, nationality, and socio-economic problems in the classroom. It is a reason that relates fundamentally to what we are trying to do through education—help youngsters understand and live the democratic way of life. What an opportunity these problems of relationships give a teacher to contrast ways of life! What an opportunity to put democracy into practice rather than rest content with words! It is these emotion-ridden areas like human relationships that test the extent to which democracy has roots in the life of the student."

"Want to open discussion now?" asked the workshop leader.

The panel members nodded. Ann then asked, "You three seem to be in agreement that intercultural education is one of the 'musts' for the high school. I'd certainly go along with you. But do we all agree on why it is needed? It seems to me that you might each advocate quite different ways of looking at intercultural education if you see quite different reasons for stressing human relationships."

"Such as?"

"Well, if you stress the problems that students now face, you might take up only those problems of student relationships which have become obvious with individual students or in group situations in your school. If you stress the broad social problems as the only reason for learning about human relationships, students in your classes might study fair employment practices or housing or races of man. But will you then be sure that such broad social problems are important to the student? If you relate everything to values and to achieving a philosophy, you have a third angle which I know is important but of which the content, I must admit, is none too clear to me."

But it was another workshop member who touched off the day's more pyrotechnic verbal fireworks: ". . . and I'm not too sure whether intercultural education is as important an area of experience as, let us say, physics or some other subject that disciplines your thinking. . ." Ideas came fast and sometimes furiously, until finally the discussion had to be stopped for lunch. That afternoon, in a talk scheduled by the planning committee, the workshop leader, a curriculum worker from the university that was co-sponsoring the workshop with the Middletown city system, offered some extended last words on the matter. Ann listened hard and applied the ideas to her efforts to foster democratic human relations in the school in which she taught.

The workshop staff member said: "Most of you agree that intercultural education and certain other centers of experience are essential to a contemporary high school program. Yet, as you also point out, they gain entrance with the greatest difficulty. Then—

"How can we tell what are important centers of experience for the high school curriculum?

"What are the high schools now teaching that makes the introduction of those essential experiences so difficult?

"To determine the important curricular experiences for today's high school student, some educators turn to the social realities of contemporary civilization as the primary source. Others find the source of curricular experiences in the needs of adolescents. Still others, who regard the development of a philosophy of life as basic, advocate the selection of those curricular experiences which throw light on conflicting value choices. In other words, one school of thought finds the primary source of curricular experiences in social realities, another finds it in the needs of adolescents, and a third chooses whatever learning experiences best contrast ways of life and values.

"Each blind man who tried to describe the elephant, it will be recalled, claimed to know the only true shape of the beast. I hope my friends on the panel will not refuse to speak to me tomorrow when I say that we saw something of that this morning when the panel dealt with intercultural education. All believe that intercultural relationships are important. Yet each found a different reason for their importance. Actually each of these reasons is important, and each explanation of the source of desirable curricular experiences is inadequate and incomplete if taken in isolation.

"A curriculum based only on needs, or only on social realities, or only on formulating a philosophy just will not do. We cannot have learning experiences which leave out student needs and problems, for these are essential if any learning is to take place. Nor can we afford experiences which ignore the culture in which we live, the social realities of our time; a grip on an understanding of these, too, is essential if we are even to exist in this complex society made up of what the sociologists like to call persons-in-culture. Nor can we neglect the constant development and practice of a philosophy of life, which is crucial if young people are to have a sense of direction rather than to drift aimlessly.

"Educators today can venture an answer to our first question: 'How can we tell what are important centers of experience for the high school curriculum?' Centers of experience for high school students can grow only from the three curricular sources, all of which interact—the needs of adolescents, the social realities of the culture, and the democratic philosophy which gives us our sense of direction. A close reading of the curricular specialists of the past two decades will indicate that, unlike the blind men, each school of thought is willing to admit that other sources than the one selected as of the greatest importance play a significant role.

"To decide, then, what centers of experience the program of the modern high school should include—intercultural, or international, or consumer, or health, or vocational, or psychological, or any other particular kind of education—we must ask ourselves whether such experiences are based on needs, throw light on social realities, and help the student steadily to develop a philosophy.

"In our quest for the most essential learning experiences for high school students, let us look at the social realities of our contemporary culture. Let us ask what kind of world we are living in. If we would determine whether intercultural experiences, for instance, are essential, we should ask ourselves whether the problem of establishing decent human relationships and of minimizing hatred, hostility, and prejudice is not one of the basic tasks in today's pattern of social realities. We should ask whether the experiences we encourage will help youngsters to understand the intercultural conflicts, trends, and problems of our culture.

"But, while we seek answers to these questions, we should remember that to determine desirable experiences for the education of high school students we must do more than examine social realities. Some social realities may as yet be beyond the ken of high school pupils. If we are going to make any impact on the attitudes of youth and avoid meaningless expenditure of breath, we must be familiar with the actual problems, concerns, and needs of the adolescents who are the heirs to this culture. One might rightly make a plea to educators to help teen-agers to solve their pressing life problems because dealing wisely and effectively with their problems is essential to achieving intelligent adjustment, responsible citizenship, or whatever similar goals are most prized by the individual educator. But, even if the case for meeting adolescent needs is argued on no higher basis than the possibility of communicating any idea or attitude or way of believing whatsoever, is it not obvious that the educator must deal with the real problems of youngsters whom he, ostensibly, is educating? Again, if we believe certain experiences to be important, we should ask ourselves whether these experiences grow from the real and vital problems of the youngsters whom we are trying to educate. For instance, if the intercultural education we foster is not related to the students' drives, tensions, and concerns, we'd better shut up shop. For people learn only what they live and and they cannot truly learn what does not matter to them.

"And are the student's experiences used to develop his viewpoint on life and to give him opportunities to practice our chosen democratic way of living? We do not want students simply to learn facts about bigotry and prejudice or any other social realities and then stay neutral toward them. We reject a limp cynicism; our adolescents have to develop and apply a positive philosophy, since a philosophy is our only source of direction.

"We cannot dodge the issue of developing a philosophy by vaguely stating our purpose to be 'meeting needs' or 'growth in relationships.' Growth must be toward a certain desirable quality of relationship. As the totalitarians have well taught us, growth may be directed toward totalitarian as well as toward democratic goals. Similarly, we have only to think of the need of the old soak for a drink or the need of a bully to punch the innocent bystander in the nose to realize how far we are from aiming to meet any and all needs. We both select and direct needs in the light of our values, be they authoritarian or democratic. Meeting needs and learning about social realities without developing an accompanying sense of direction can only produce chaotic thinking. Intercultural education that does not come to grips with an understanding of the democratic way of life is Hamlet played without the melancholy Dane himself.

"Yet, too often at present, experiences which will meet needs, illuminate social realities, and develop values can only smuggle their way into current high school curriculums. Urgent and undeniable as the grass which forces itself between pavement cracks on a busy city street, they merely take root in extracurricular activities, optional or free choice courses, or in clubs, or work their way into the occasional interstices between ivy-covered traditional subject matter. They sometimes infiltrate into the established and respectable subjects only to produce odd, hybrid blossoms—as, for instance, when a class hears about intercultural relationships through a study of ancient Rome, or when a student encounters personal or health or consumer problems through some tortured distortion in grammar or intermediate algebra or chemisty classes. Is this the best we can do to make high school education vital and to center it on life problems?

"In America we keep saying that we hold to the democratic way of life and that we are for education for all American youth. Yet, save for many honorable exceptions, in community after community a high school designed for the elite still carries on an education appropriate for the eighteenth-century British aristocrat, if for anyone. Grammar and Greek history; classics, cosines, and conjugations; frog dissection (which is a relative newcomer!) and French; Shakespeare and chivalry; elegant lettering and English literature; binomial theorems, the rise of Phoenicia, for ever and ever, amen. From the teacher point of view, it is mine not to reason why, mine but to teach a subject matter which some obscure destiny once dictated. From the student point of view, it is mine not to reason why, mine but to absorb mechanically, give back phonographically, and wait for the bell. For both teacher and student, life begins at 3:30.

"Have inroads on this conception of education been made in the American high school? Of course they have; we can all cite evidence. And more power to those who are trying to bring actual life and the American high school into their proper relationships! But my portrait of the problem, unfortunately, is all too close to the actual situation in too many American high schools.

"The confusion in the American high school comes about because the new is struggling to be born and the old refuses to lie down to die and be buried."

To at least one listener, Ann Smith, teacher of social studies in the West High School, the talk summed up the problems she was facing in developing intercultural experiences in her school. She felt sure that she could document the importance of intercultural education for West High. Prejudice, discrimination, and bigotry were woven into the social fabric of the community in which she lived and worked. As a real problem of the student body, it showed itself in a dozen obvious ways; in the social-economic discrimination which marked elections to club membership; in drugstore table cliques; in the rudeness of some minority group members; in the obsequious, studied politeness with which still others reacted to discrimination; in the lifted eyebrow and meaningful exchange of smiles during the reading of literature that contained stereotypes of Jews; in the embarrassment with which a second-generation youngster waited for the substitute teacher's inevitable mispronunciation of his name; in the expressed gratification of some students at not going to East High where so many Negroes went; in the loose use of slurring epithets; in scurrilous jingles popular for the moment. If America really meant its education to help the young to understand and practice the democratic way of life, such social and personal problems—the ones that really count—were the raw material for the making and application of a philosophy.

To Ann it was evident that the extension of democratic human relationships was an integral phase of democratic education. The need was inescapable. The major question seemed to be which approaches were most fruitful. But all this was not so self-evident to many others on the West High staff.

*◄§ Toward Democratic Human Relations was first delivered as a
talk in the Great Human Issues of Our Times series of George Peabody College for Teachers. The series itself, addresses by faculty
members from the outdoor stage on summer evenings before a large
proportion of the student body, was launched in 1951 as a contribution to musically opulent but intellectually malnourished summer
cultural events.*

*Quite possibly more people who heard me that night in Nashville,
Tennessee, in 1956 disagreed with much of my viewpoint than
agreed. Yet the highly varied audience, largely students from every
Southern state, heard me out with courtesy and attention. Long after
the floodlights had gone out upon the speakers' platform, small clus-
ters of people kept on talking animatedly on campus and in the
town. Someone could turn off the lights over the speakers' platform
but no one could turn off the problem of race relations over the
South. The problem just wouldn't go away.*

16 *Toward Democratic Human Relations*

In America today we face a tremendous challenge, the challenge
to foster in this nation good human relations among people of
varied religious, racial, and nationality backgrounds. We are
Americans all. We came from everywhere on the face of the
earth. We intend to remain here in these United States. Together we live and together we must live well.

Fortunately, as we build toward better human relations, we
have the support of four major World Ideas. Democracy, religion, science, and law are on the side of those who work toward
better relationships among people who are different in religious
preferences, skin pigment, and ancestral background. Let us look
afresh at these four verbal symbols which represent man's vital
World Ideas. Take democracy first.

The peddlers of prejudice can derive no comfort from the documents of democracy. When our ancestors wrote the Declaration of Independence, they said, "All men are created equal." The word they used was "all." As the superintendent of schools of Nashville reminded the City Teachers Association in an able speech on desegregation, the Declaration of Independence has never been amended. When the Founding Fathers developed an enduring Constitution of the United States at Philadelphia, they began, "We the people." All of us belong to "we the people" and second-class citizenship has no place in the American way of living. To make sure, we later added a fourteenth amendment, "No State shall make or enforce any law which shall abridge the privileges or immunities of citizens of the United States; nor shall any State deprive any person of life, liberty, or property, without due process of law; nor deny to any person within its jurisdiction the equal protection of its laws."

An American historian, James Truslow Adams, summed up the American democratic dream as ". . . that dream of a land in which whole life should be better and richer and fuller for every man, with opportunity for each according to his ability and achievement." The key word is "every." "It has been a dream of being able to grow to fullest development as man and woman, unhampered by the barriers which had been slowly erected in older civilizations, unrepressed by social orders which had developed for the benefit of classes rather than for the simple human being of any and every class." There is no room in the land of the American dream for a caste system.

The democratic creed includes respect for individual personality, working together for common purposes commonly arrived at, and the use of the method of intelligence. No matter how thin the peddlers of prejudice slice their logic, they cannot reconcile discriminatory practices with our democratic way of life.

Religion is a second World Idea which supports the improvement of human relations. The powerful Judaic-Christian tradition of western civilization affirms human brotherhood. The religious leadership of the western world agrees on one God, the Universal Father, not a conglomeration of quarreling Greek gods, each with a personal following. Such a Universal Father can hardly be expected to maintain separate but equal heavens. Many religions add that man has an immortal soul. It is difficult for a believer in the soul to credit that the souls of those whose ancestors came to America by steerage in the nineteenth century are somehow inferior to the souls of those whose ancestors came earlier to America on the Mayflower. It is interesting to notice that those who attempt the impossible feat of reconciling religion and racism never quote Jesus, but instead restrict themselves to Genesis. Christian and Jewish religious tenets are incompatible with prejudice and discrimination.

Science is a third World Idea which supports better human relations. The evidence from science that racism is rot and stereotyping is simple-minded is especially significant when we recognize, with Otto Klineberg, that post-Darwinian science made vigorous attempts to establish innate superiority of one or another group. But psychologists tell us that no tests have been devised which prove the innate or biologically built-in superiority in native intelligence of groups of one color, or religious persuasion, or geographical locality. Culture, which is learned, always enters into the responses. The geneticists add that only a small part of the potential development of human beings has yet taken place on this planet.

Painstakingly, the semanticists remind us that Catholic *one* is not Catholic *two*, that Negro *one* is not Negro *two*, that Southerner *one* is not Southerner *two*. Grouping each as identical is an abuse of man's power of communication. Stubbornly, the students of the human body remind us that they have discovered blood types common to all mankind, but that they are unable to isolate Methodist blood, or Baptist blood, or Church of Christ blood, or Jewish blood, or Italian blood, or white blood. However, they have discovered the somewhat shocking fact that all of us have colored blood—red colored.

In addition to all else that they have taught us about race and culture, the anthropologists advise us not to be ethnocentric. When we inquire as to what they mean, they tell us a legend common among many brown peoples, including the Athabasca Indians and the inhabitants of the Malay peninsula. The legend has it that the All Powerful, having some time on his hands, decided to make man. He shaped the clay and placed it in the oven. But unfortunately he let man bake too long, as cooks have been known to do, and the product was a black man, burned to a crisp. So the All Powerful cast him away and the black man went to Africa. The All Powerful tried again and this time was overly cautious, for he pulled out of the oven a pale-faced man, quite underdone and scarcely baked. So the All Powerful, displeased, tossed away this man too and the pale man went to Europe where temporarily he enjoyed remarkable success. But on the third attempt—you guessed it—the All Powerful baked a man who was just right, a rich, golden brown, an ideally handsome man who looked exactly like the people who tell this legend. The ideal, golden brown man lived happily ever after in his part of the world. The moral is: don't confuse ethnocentrism, one of mankind's bad habits, with reasoned thought.

Many are the civilizations which regarded themselves as the conquerors, the chosen ones, the master people. But now in the world history books they rank three short lines each. The poet Percy Bysshe Shelley wrote the obituary of such self-styled master races in *Ozymandias:*

I met a traveler from an antique land
Who said: Two vast and trunkless legs of stone
Stand in the desert. Near them, on the sand,
Half sunk, a shattered visage lies, whose frown,
And wrinkled lip, and sneer of cold command,
Tell that its sculptor well those passions read
Which yet survive, stamped on these lifeless things,
The hand that mocked them, and the heart that fed:
And on the pedestal these words appear:
'My name is Ozymandias, king of kings:
Look on my works, ye Mighty, and despair!'
Nothing beside remains. Round the decay
Of that colossal wreck, boundless and bare
The lone and level sands stretch far away.

The fourth of the great World Ideas supporting the improvement of human relations is the law. Like a giant, the law moves with slow, steady majesty. The milestones along the giant's way include: the Magna Carta, the English Bill of Rights, the legal heritage of the French and American Revolutions. In America, the milestones include: the Mayflower Compact, the Bill of Rights and the Constitution, the Emancipation Proclamation, and the nineteenth century trio of amendments forbidding slavery, fostering equal protection of the laws, and specifying that the right of citizens to vote shall not be denied.

In our own times, the law spoke again through a United States Supreme Court ruling of May 17, 1954:

"In these days, it is doubtful that any child may be expected to succeed in life if he is denied the opportunity of an education. Such an opportunity, where the state has undertaken to provide it, is a right which must be made available to all on equal terms.

"We come then to the question presented: Does segregation of the children in public schools solely on the basis of race, even though the physical facilities and other 'tangible' factors may be equal, deprive the children of the minority group of equal educational opportunities? We believe that it does. . . In the field of public education the doctrine of 'separate but equal' has no place. Separate educational facilities are inherently unequal."

"But," one may inquire, "how about state and local laws which support racial discrimination in public education?" One year after the 1954 decision, the Court spoke again in a decree:

"These cases were decided on May 17, 1954. The opinions of that day . . . declaring the fundamental principle that racial discrimination in public education is unconstitutional, are incorporated herein by reference. All provisions of federal, state, or local law requiring or permitting such discrimination must yield to this principle."

For years prior to the Supreme Court decision, conscience had battled segregation of students in public schools. Conscience had the better of the moral argument on the ideological battlefields of democracy, religion, and science. Now in the mid-fifties of the twentieth century, the Constitution of the United States has joined conscience in a powerful alliance. Conscience and the law of the land each say that the public schools are to be open to all on equal terms.

So, in the United States of America, the question is no longer whether or not to continue segregated public education. The law is clear. Racial discrimination in public education is against the law of the land.

The question of "whether" is settled and finished. The live questions today are "how" and "when."

Democracy, religion, science, and the law are the great World Ideas of our times. These deep-rooted, ancient forces underwrite the eventual triumph of better human relations among men. But you and I, living in the stream of history, do not inhabit any eventual tomorrow. We live today, right here, in the world and the nation and the South. We are educators, not statesmen, not ministers, not scientists, not lawyers. We are committed by our calling to contribute what we can to building decent, friendly, humane relations among men. What can we do, here and now?

We can educate. We can accept our responsibility for intercultural education in our schools. Some may say that the contributions of each of us are as drops in the bucket. But drops of water made the Grand Canyon and the Falls of Yellowstone.

If, as teachers, we accept our responsibility to educate for better human relations, we may help make a better world internationally. The world is looking to the United States for moral leadership, for new expertness in human relations.

Let us never make the mistake of assuming that there are only two camps in today's world: the Western powers and the Soviet Communist powers. There exists a third camp, larger than either of the two mentioned. These are the neutrals, the uncommitted who live by the millions in Southeastern Asia, in the islands of Oceania, in India, in the Middle East, across an awakening Africa.

Turn the microscope carefully on these people who are vital to our future. What is their prevailing skin color? It is darker than that of the majority of Americans. Inescapably, these neutrals judge the United States by our race relations. A racial incident which is carried on the eighth page of our local newspaper at home, if at all, is a front-page story in Singapore, Saigon, Calcutta, Beirut, and Cairo. Like it or not, the sheer, tough fact of life is that our problems of human relations are problems of international concern, woven into our destiny as a world power.

To the neutrals, the democratic way of life is on trial and manifestations of undemocratic human relations in the United States constitute exhibit "A" for the prosecution. The prosecution, specifically the Communists, will lose no opportunity to remind the neutrals of our lapses. The neutrals, and indeed many in our own camp too, are asking, "Uncle Sam, which do you really mean? Do you mean the noble and glowing words about democracy as a way of life—respect for individual personality, working together for common purposes commonly arrived at, using the method of intelligence? Or do you mean the undemocratic practices in human relations reported to us? Uncle Sam, you can't have it both ways." If all the world knew an old Anglo-Saxon recreation known as "poker," it might add, "Uncle Sam, the time has come to put up or close up!"

We are American educators. Will we put up or will we close up? If we have the courage and the insight to put up through intercultural education, we will have helped Uncle Sam in his rendezvous with destiny on the world scene. If we close up, through fear, we speed the march of the Communist boots. As Elmer Davis reminded us, we can't be the land of the free without also being the home of the brave.

Intercultural education is necessary not only because we are American educators who are conscious of the tides of world opinion. We are also American educators who live in the South and who have a responsibility for the education of our people. The Supreme Court decision and decree of 1954 and 1955 hit the South like a bolt from the blue. The Solid South of history became at least three Souths. One South moved officially toward compliance with the decisions: Delaware, Maryland, West Virginia, Kentucky, Missouri, and Oklahoma. Another South followed the policy of "wait and see": Tennessee, Florida, Arkansas, and Texas. A third South actively and officially resisted the decisions: Louisiana, Mississippi, Alabama, Georgia, South Carolina, North Carolina, and Virginia. To complicate matters even more, in each of the Souths there was a wide variation of local conditions from community to community.

It is little wonder that many Southerners of many persuasions cried out for more time. It is little wonder that the far-seeing among them also cried out for more education in human relations.

But time is to use, not for standing still. Education is for clarifications which replace confusions, for reasoned reflection. Desperately needed is the healing power of discussion, of communication, of sober consideration of alternatives. This the educators, rather than the politicians, can foster. Courts and lawyers, politicians and legislatures can rule on segregation or desegregation. But it is the educators who have the day-to-day responsibility for fostering better human relations through education. Educators are the humble, undramatic people who must keep the channels of communication open, support mankind's hard-earned values, develop the use of intelligence. Educators are the quiet people who must pick up the pieces even while the shouting and struggling of the extremists goes on.

In a society in which better human relations are supported by the four great World Ideas and at a time when the situation in our world, our nation, and our South demands that we not falter, a renewed stress on education for mutual understanding seems inevitable. An examination of the development of education for better human relations, promising practices, and research-based insights should be useful to all citizens, and especially to educators who must increasingly develop skills on the human relations frontier.

First came the missionary stage. During the 1920's and early 30's, a few men of good will stumped the country, calling for more emphasis upon teaching human understanding through American schools. But Americans were busy with what Charles A. Beard called "the golden glow of prosperity," when a presidential candidate could run on the slogan "two chickens in every pot and two cars in every garage." The ugly Ku Klux Klan was only a footnote in the history of the fabulous twenties. So people did not pay much heed to the intercultural missionaries.

Next came the stage of the simple answers. Some of the people who listened to the intercultural missionaries struck on hunches. So some teachers encouraged pageants in which students dressed up in the costumes of their ancestral relatives. High was the hope that everlasting love for the Chinese laundryman would thus automatically be insured. There was a great vogue for George Washington Carver and his peanuts. The simple answer was that if only white children could hear about what Dr. Carver had done with the lowly peanut, human brotherhood would be established across the land. Others put their faith in inspirational lectures. Some adopted the simple answer that all that people needed was acquaintance with the bare facts of science. The suggested answers were simple—too simple.

Then something happened in the world which forced intercultural education to come of age. The free societies found that they had to take fascism seriously. The Fascist armies marched and counter-marched, and the little nations began to go down. We came to realize that Mussolini, bellowing and braying on the balconies of Rome, meant it when he said "We or they"; that Adolf Hitler, with animal-like hysteria in his voice, meant it when he screamed that today it was Deutschland but tomorrow the world. Many Americans came to grips with what democracy meant and recognized that the Master Race theory could be no part of the democratic dream. Other Americans, less philosophical, simply recognized the brute need for unity among Americans in a time of war. The need came home to all Americans one hot, summer day in Detroit when the arsenal of democracy stopped dead while whites and blacks went looting and killing and rioting down the broad boulevards of the city.

Taking fascism seriously, citizens and educators invested new energy and funds in human relations education. Intercultural education came of age as it entered the stage of promising practices. Workshops in human relations education multiplied. Consultation and research in school systems were sponsored by strengthened organizations. Yearbooks of professional organizations and complete issues of magazines were given over to the reporting of promising practices. Pamphlets were prepared; resource units were developed. Simple answers gave way to promising practices as American educators moved from hunches to tryouts and observation.

First among the promising approaches is building better human relations through a democratic atmosphere in the school and in the home—an atmosphere of belongingness, of mutual affection, of being wanted, of having a place in the scheme of things. Such an atmosphere is the polar opposite of a climate of fear, mistrust, hostility, suspicion. In the building of a democratic atmosphere the elementary school teacher plays a crucial role, for every bigot was once a child.

A second and allied promising practice is the study of children and youth to deal better with their tensions, anxieties, and insecurities. So human relations-minded teachers keep anecdotal records, work on case studies, and make sociograms. They recognize that bullies may become haters, that the name-caller may adopt other epithets when he grows older, that the picked-on child may become the scapegoat, or, in reaction, the aggressor. With the discovery of how children differ, come classrooms which are seed beds for better human relations, schoolrooms marked by planning, sharing, the relaxation of absurd uniform expectancies.

A third approach introduces into the lives of the young people those books which deal in an honest and friendly fashion with minority groups. Our libraries are growing rich in such books. Slowly they are replacing the books about exotic customs which persuade children that minority group members are strange and queer and probably a little bit crazy.

A fourth promising practice is to focus on the immediate problems of human relations of schools. The slogan "Brotherhood begins on your own block," makes good sense. How about sportsmanship toward the visiting basketball teams rather than gallery references to Polacks and Wops? How about seeing that school elections are not dominated by youngsters from one particular side of the tracks? Do the rural youngsters boarding a bus feel discriminated against as urban youngsters stay on for extracurricular activities? The school of which an administrator says blandly, "We have no problems here," often houses unrecognized problems.

Fifth of the promising practices is the two-way passage between school and community. The divorce between what goes on inside the school building and what goes on in the outer community is tragic. Outside of the school there are hundreds of potential teachers who would be delighted to be asked in to help: the G. I. just back from the Orient, the housewife who knows a particular skill, the workman who could describe his job, the religious leader who could describe his church, the minority group member who could describe something on which he happens to be expert, not necessarily the contributions or problems of his own cultural or racial group. Outside the school, awaiting visitation by the youngsters, are stores and factories and institutions manned by people of varied backgrounds. For still more enterprising educators, there are opportunities for young people of varied backgrounds to work together to improve the community through repainting the recreation room of the settlement house, clearing a vacant lot for play space, finding common cause with the young of many backgrounds.

A sixth opportunity for education for better human relations is through extracurricular activities. An English teacher need not always direct hokum like "Minnie's Mad Monday" selected from a catalogue of plays. There are thoughtful plays about human relationships, and Mother and Father and all the neighbors will still turn out in large numbers. Forums can bring together youngsters of varied backgrounds to talk on "What America Means to Me" and on live social issues. Athletic events are a great common denominator; as a youngster put it, "What is the difference about his nationality or race as long as he can pitch?" Many are the opportunities for human relations education in extracurricular activities.

A seventh promising practice is to permeate the regular subjects of the curriculum with opportunities for intercultural understanding. In art there exists an opportunity to help young people to see that all peoples have contributed to art—not simply those of one nationality, one religion, one race. The subject matter of history is replete with opportunities to learn about human relationships. One large school system listed twenty major topics for intercultural emphasis in American History, including European colonization of America, treatment of the American Indian, religious differences, immigration, sectionalism and slavery, attitude toward colonial possessions, etc. Literature is largely about human relationships. Science enables us to deal with heredity, environment, the facts of race. The study of world languages affords an opportunity to become acquainted with the cultures of people, as well as with their grammar. Business education can deal with problems of discrimination in employment, as well as teach the business skills.

Many of the best modern schools use an eighth approach as their instruction focuses on centers of experiences, the real problems of young people in a democratic society. Units deal with health, recreation, vocations, public opinion, labor-management relationships. Problems of human relationships are an integral part of such realistic units. Take the study of housing, for instance. A student cannot study housing for long without coming up against problems of discrimination, of gentlemen's agreements, of slums, and of restrictions.

The ninth and last promising practice which will be mentioned here is one which some people mistakenly believe to be all of intercultural education. Actually, the direct approach through units on prejudice, conflicts among generations, race, or religion is only one phase of a broad program of education for better human relations.

Probably even more significant than the development of promising practices is the current stage of research to determine the best insights. In the 1950's, teams of scholars are carrying on interdisciplinary research into prejudice and its treatment at great university centers and through human relations agencies. No report on research on human relations can yet be definitive, but the hypotheses being explored may at least be stated.

As to prejudice, recent research points to two major sources. One source of prejudice is repeated frustration of the individual. If a person is denied his basic needs for recognition and affection, if he finds himself continuously blocked, if his sense of worth and personal adequacy is denied, he is likely to develop a personality structure characterized by fear, hate, and aggression. So his prejudice is a reflection of a sickness within himself.

A second source of prejudice is cultural learning. Suppose the society which surrounds the individual takes prejudice for granted. Then the individual lives in a pattern of discrimination and takes for granted the stereotypes about inferiority which he hears. Without examining the matter, he adopts the attitudes about him as his own. He learns his prejudice from his surroundings.

How can we meet prejudices which stem from frustration and which stem from cultural learnings? The researchers are beginning to identify the better insights for human relations education.

An essential which is reaffirmed is the creation of a democratic atmosphere designed to reduce the personal insecurities and tensions of children. The forces of scientific research are increasingly backing the popular rediscovery of acceptance and belongingness —in short, of love. One of the major concepts of modern educators can no longer be dismissed as a sentimental notion.

Another insight testifies to the power of intergroup contacts in situations involving cooperation. Note the last word. Contact alone is not enough. To understand and accept other people, we must work together in situations involving common concerns. Differences grow less important when we work together for better schools, housing, health, neighborhoods.

The researchers enjoy titling another insight "emotional sensitization to other intercultural groups" or "empathy." Translated, this means helping people put themselves in the other person's shoes. Fiction, movies, radio, television, and recordings can help us to recognize that there, but for the grace of God, go I.

If a person is to discover the inconsistency or invalidity of some of his existing attitudes, digging out the facts for himself helps. People do not change through being lectured at. They are more likely to change when they become data-gatherers who analyze school and community conditions through surveys and action research. No one can reconstruct another person's values for him. A person who obtains data and lives with the facts must engage in his own reflection on his values.

One final insight from current research throws doubt on the old saw used to defend the status quo, "You can't legislate good human relations." It is true that laws bring no overnight changes in attitudes. But attitudes are learned in social situations. When we reduce discriminatory practices in areas like employment or in education, we reduce the potential for learning prejudice. Some urge that changing the environment through democratic law is one of the greatest contributions to good human relations that can be made. When the social supports of democratic behavior are shored up, the cultural matrix in which we live and in which children grow up is improved. Education and legislation together make a better society.

In this last half of the twentieth century, the frontier of education for better human relations lies before each of us. If through fears or pressures, we fail in this educational responsibility—but we will not fail. The four great World Ideas support us. The world, the nation and the section demand that we not fail.

If we can build better human relations through American schools, the awful vision of Mr. Whittle will not come true. Mr. Whittle is a mild-mannered college professor in a novel by Robert Nathan called *Mr. Whittle and the Morning Star*. One morning Mr. Whittle wakes with the vision that mankind is doomed.

"You had everything, he cried out silently; all that was needed was for your hearts to keep up with your heads. Think how far you went in science and discovery; you were masters of earth and air. Even the pox had given in to you; you had conquered disease, hunger, heat and cold, distance, silence, and the desert. There remained only fear, hate, and death; and these have finally done you in. . . .

"You were gods; from the point of view of an ant, or a spaniel, your powers were so tremendous as to appear divine. Truly, you harnessed the lightning, you made use of elements, you discovered the firmament, and invented music. There was nothing you could not do, nothing that was too much for you, except to get along with yourselves and with each other. That was the one thing that was out of the question. . . .

"Man himself became your enemy, for a number of reasons . . . because of the length of his nose or the color of his hair, because he had more money than you, or because he had less . . . for the slightest of reasons, or for no reason at all. That was the end of you; for you forgot that you, too, were man."

Let us so teach our young that they never forget that they too belong to man.

◄§ The Nashville Story *which was published in 1958 is, I hope, dispassionate. Living the experience was anything but. Working toward school integration in a Southern community has little resemblance to the polite indignation, the easy verbal solutions, and the unanimity of gatherings of intellectuals in the North.*

When you work on race problems in the South, you are engaged in no parlor game for living room liberals. You are playing for keeps. After a meeting on integration you may feel melodramatic and faintly foolish when you lower the blinds to minimize possible flying glass from the picture window should an extremist throw a rock. But you lower the blinds. You may feel like a member of the democratic underground when you park your car several blocks from the church where the integration meeting is to be held. But with all too clear recall of the tires ripped with an ice pick the night before, you park blocks away.

17 *The Nashville Story*

THIS is an account of some undramatic Nashville citizens trying to help their Southern community toward integration of public schools. The story takes place in no man's land. Between compliance and resistance lies Tennessee, a "wait and see" state.

The Supreme Court decision was announced in 1954 and everyone seemed to wait. Men and women of good will in Nashville waited too. Surely somebody would do something about it. It takes quite a while before a person of good will realizes that what he is waiting for is himself.

In the spring of 1955, the local presidents of the United Church Women and the Council of Jewish Women agreed that something should be done to educate the community on the Court's decision. So they invited 13 additional community organizations to co-sponsor a workshop. Seven organizations accepted: American Association of University Women, B'nai B'rith, Citizens Committee for the Public Schools, Council of Colored Parents and Teachers, League of Women Voters of Nashville, Nashville Association of Churches, Young Women's Christian Association.

Presidents are loaded down with responsibilities, so a trio of women handled many details. After the workshop, someone said, "Were you three chosen to represent a balance of religions and races?" The trio happened to be Catholic, Protestant, and Jewish; two white and one Negro. The matter of "balance" had occurred to no one, least of all to the three. A job needed to be done.

The sponsors had anticipated 150 in attendance at the evening meeting in May 1955. Instead, 500 came to hear Whitworth Stokes III, a local attorney; Charles S. Johnson, the president of Fisk University; and George Mitchell, the director of the Southern Regional Council. The three men spoke on "The Supreme Court Decision and Its Meaning for Our Community." The next day, 180 people came back for the experience of communication through small groups across racial lines. The writer, a professor at the local teachers college, served as moderator of both meetings. The meetings were held in the Jewish Community Center; clergymen of the various faiths spoke the invocation. About two-thirds of the participants were white; seating was unsegregated.

But a workshop, however effective, is soon over. Some religiously motivated people stepped into the gap. Typical were a teacher at a college for Christian workers and a head of a commission for a Protestant denomination. Luncheons for discussion and fellowship were held at intervals and attended by leaders of both races. Out of the sharing grew two goals, another community workshop and a permanent community organization on human relations.

The sponsors of the February 1956 workshop had grown from 9 to 26 organizations, including labor, nursing, and church groups. Now the topic was "Integration—How and When?" Now the workshop was held in a Protestant church. Now school experience from outside the community was called on; school-

Men from Baltimore and St. Louis, Harry Bard and Frank Sskwor, talked to 600 people and held an off-the-record conference with local superintendents and school board members. Back the next night came 360 to work out recommendations to sponsoring organizations for follow-up action. As moderator, the writer can testify that the meetings were orderly and thoughtful.

The next objective was to establish a community organization to work toward better group relationships. More than a dedicated few would be needed if Nashville were to have an effective permanent group on human relations. Still more Nashvillians who were white, Protestant, and of "old" families in Nashville must accept a greater lead in human relations work if the new organization were to really make a difference.

Our faithful few approached community leaders, requesting them to join the sponsoring group; 84 community leaders agreed to sponsor an organizational meeting. In April 1956, with more than 120 people in attendance, the Nashville Community Relations Conference was formally born.

Responsibility was lodged in the hands of established Nashville community leaders. The five officers were the president of a local foundry and machine company, an attorney who was the son and grandson of Tennessee lawyers, a head of a university department of medicine, a state PTA officer, the wife of a Negro college president, and an active community worker of the Jewish faith. A 50-person Board of Directors and a 13-person Executive Committee, biracial, multi-religioned, and active in business, labor and the professions, were created. Later, 11 committees were set up to tap the energies of still more members: membership; finances; meetings; fact-finding; parent education; fellowship luncheons; community education; human relations education in the schools; health; religious activities; employment.

In August 1956 a letter from the Executive Committee to the Nashville School Board, which was being sued by Negro parents, urged school board members to formulate a plan to desegregate in the fall of 1956. "Only in one respect do we make any suggestion—we would much prefer that you, as the local authority, develop and install the plan rather than have the United States Courts order some plan of compliance." The vice-president of the Conference appeared before the board in support of the letter.

The school board took no action toward desegregation till the fall term began. But October 30, 1956, the headlines read, "City Schools Act to Integrate Next Fall."

One of the active committees of the Nashville Community Relations Conference was the committee on human relations education in the schools, made up of respected educators from Nashville colleges and universities. The Conference committee offered help to the superintendent of schools through a letter in December 1956. While the offer was never officially accepted, members of the committee cooperated informally with school administrators.

The Conference committee on parent education made efforts to persuade the local PTA's of white schools to hold meetings in preparation for the coming desegregation. Committee efforts were unsuccessful because of the unreadiness of the white PTA Council to foster meetings of any type concerning desegregation.

The Conference committee on community education was influential particularly through the activities of its chairman who quietly consulted with the transportation authorities on bus desegregation and with the police department on meeting possible violence. The committee on fact-finding reported on the extent of desegregation in Nashville organizations and institutions. The Fellowship Luncheons included a tribute to the late president of Fisk University and a panel through which spokesmen for Nashville organizations described how desegregation of their memberships had been achieved.

By New Year's Day, 1957, concern of those who were working for better human relations in Nashville shifted to the coming session of the Tennessee legislature. Would the general assembly pass segregationist legislation?

After lengthy sessions, the Executive Committee decided to develop a statement on 1957 school legislation which advanced many reasons for its conclusions, "we firmly believe that no legislation on this subject should be passed at this session of the Tennessee General Assembly." Copies of the mimeographed statement of several pages were distributed to each legislator, brought to the Governor, sent to the various media of communication.

Meanwhile, Governor Clement proposed two bills, described as "moderate segregation" legislation. One bill authorized boards of education to provide separate schools for white and Negro children whose parents voluntarily elected to send them to such schools. The second bill gave boards of education the power to assign pupils to schools for a variety of reasons.

Two conferences were held with the Governor in which he explained his position to representatives of the Conference, who remained unpersuaded of the desirability of any legislation. The Conference, however, did not testify as an organization[1] against the "moderate segregation" legislation proposed by Governor Clement. Some Executive Committee members, impressed by the vehemence of the extremists, argued that the Governor's bills were the best that could be expected under the circumstances and predicted that they would be found unconstitutional anyway.

At the public hearing of the Senate and House Education and Judiciary committees of the Tennessee General Assembly on January 15, 1957, a clergyman of the Southern Baptist faith and the writer of this article were the only two white people in Tennessee heard in testimony against the bills. Both of us testified as individuals, not as representatives of our employers or organizations. The bills passed overwhelmingly in mid-January 1957.[2]

[1] Basically, the Conference conceives of itself as an educational organization, not a pressure group. This orientation will probably be reinforced by another 1957 law passed by the Tennessee General Assembly requiring organizations attempting to influence legislation on segregation and integration to register. By the deadline set for registration, no organization of any persuasion registered.

[2] From the date of passage, the two laws were constantly cited by segregationists as they pressured the Nashville Board of Education. On September 6, 1957, Judge Miller of the Federal District Court ruled that the Tennessee law authorizing separate schools for Negro and white children whose parents voluntarily elected to send them to such schools was unconstitutional "on its face." On February 18, 1958, the same judge disapproved the assignment law proposal and the parent-pupil preference plan as applied to Nashville. He ruled that by April 7, 1958, the Nashville School Board must adopt a "substantial" plan "and one which contemplates elimination of racial discrimination throughout the school system with all deliberate speed."

The Federal District Court, in late January 1957, accepted the Nashville School Board's proposal that desegregation of only the first grade in the Nashville public school take place in September 1957. For a period of time following this decision, the board of education and the school administration of Nashville continued the long-established policy of "wait and see" which was highly characteristic of both the city, the state, and much of the upper South. Then, in March 1957, the superintendent of schools presented to the board of education a statement calling for men of good will to support the board in carrying out the court order; the board adopted it unanimously.

In order to help the board carry out its new policy and as an indication of support from people of good will, the Nashville Community Relations Conference in May 1957 sponsored a public talk by Omer Carmichael, superintendent of schools of Louisville, Kentucky. W. A. Bass, the superintendent of schools of Nashville, an able schoolman nearing retirement, was cooperative. He invited Dr. Carmichael to speak at a morning meeting of administrators and teachers and urged the Conference to write principals advising them to send teachers to hear Dr. Carmichael at the evening meeting. At least 400 Nashville teachers heard the Louisville superintendent, and an audience of 400 attended the evening session at Hume-Fogg High School.

The superintendent of Nashville then initiated a series of meetings in the schools to explain the board's policy. The program met marked resistance from one patron who monopolized the first meeting at a school and who later organized a "Parents Preference Committee." The new segregationist committee began getting thousands of signatures to a petition "preferring" desegregated schools. Shortly afterwards the superintendent fell ill; plans lapsed for active preparation for desegregation of the first grade through community meetings sponsored by the school system.

The stark, brutal question became whether or not law and order would be maintained. During the summer of 1957, the Executive Committee of the Nashville Community Relations Conference encouraged four outstanding local business and civic leaders to sponsor a statement supporting law and order. The statement did not endorse integration; it simply called for law enforcement.

Eventually, the statement was signed by 600 people, including some Nashville community leaders whose names were known and respected. Particularly prominent among the endorsers were clergymen, educators, doctors, leaders of the Methodist Board of Education, and divinity school professors.

But businessmen proved extremely hesitant to add their signatures to the law and order statement. The Mayor indicated support but thought it inappropriate to initiate the statement by his signature. Various prominent community figures, including some eminent educators, found reasons for not signing.

Copies of the statement and lists of signatures were turned over to the superintendent of schools after a meeting in July 1957 in which the in-coming and out-going superintendents addressed and thanked the Conference.

In the last few weeks prior to desegregation of the first grade, the Conference also attempted to develop community meetings for discussion of the coming desegregation. The Conference members found that leaders of various organizations were willing to cooperate, including the League of Women Voters, the American Association of University Women, the Nashville Association of Social Workers, the Negro PTA, the Nashville Ministerial Association, the Nashville Association of Churches, etc. The plans received a fatal setback when the white PTA Council decided that meetings were inadvisable.

Meanwhile, the Tennessee Federation for Constitutional Government, which had among its key leaders a professor of English at Vanderbilt University, continued to oppose the coming desegregation. The Parents Preference Committee continued to gather signatures.

The extremist segregationists also increased their activities. Meetings of the Ku Klux Klan were held. Yet only 50 robed Klansmen attended one highly publicized meeting which the writer observed.

Shortly after the Clinton trial, John Kasper made Nashville his headquarters. He began with small audiences. With time and publicity, his audiences steadily increased. One of his final harangues was delivered with rope in hand before the state capitol of Tennessee.

On August 8, 1957, the extremists, including Kasper, appeared before the school board in opposition to the coming desegregation of the first grade. At the same meeting, the president of the Nashville Community Relations Conference indicated support of the board, asked the board how the Conference might best help, and released the law and order statement signed by 600 people.

The appearance before the board by the representative of the Nashville Community Relations Conference was one of very few moderate organizational counters to the increasing violent talk of the extremists. Though the biracial Conference represented the position of only a segment of Nashville opinion, through the Conference statements and activities the voice of conscience and humane relations among men was heard in the community. It has been said that the existence of the Conference explains partially, though certainly not wholly, why the Nashville story, 1957 version, did not become the Little Rock story, 1957 version.

The great body of Nashville citizens avoided any commitment as they followed the social strategy of "Say nothing, wait and see." But time was running out. There was a touch of September in the air. The opening of school was just around the corner.

The rest of the story the reader knows. For several days in September 1957, black headlines shrieked of Nashville in the national and world press. Racists demonstrated and threatened as 19 wide-eyed Negro six-year-olds came to formerly all-white schools. Then at 12:30 A. M. on the morning of September 10, 1957, a bomb blew up the new Hattie Cotton School. The blast blew many solid citizens of Nashville out of their comfortable beds. The city temporarily awakened from slumber.

In the morning the police cracked down on would-be demonstrators. The demonstrations dissolved. The six-year-olds went back to school and Kasper went to jail. People explained to each other that what had happened was all the fault of Kasper, that outsider from New Jersey.

In March 1958, the Jewish Community Center was dynamited by racists. The Nashville Community Relations Conference said "we believe that the citizens of this community are all partly responsible . . . to the extent that we failed to support adequately with our time, our resources and our ideas the forces in our community working for harmony, justice, equality and dignity for all our citizens. This is the time . . . to join hands in a total community effort for better human relations."

Addendum, 1961:

I concluded my article with the comment, "As to the future, including the fall of 1958, the gods give no guarantees." I am happy now to add that, following the blasts, a revulsion against school segregation extremists developed in Nashville. Though the dynamiters were never identified, school integration to date has proceeded a grade a year in an atmosphere characterized by order and restraint. As to school desegregation, moderate views supporting better human relations prevailed.

The gods have not changed their policies, however; they still give no guarantees. What happens is up to people. Edmund Burke said it well, "All that is needed for the forces of evil to triumph in the world is for enough good men to do nothing."

W. V. T.

꜒ᔥ *We left Nashville in 1957 for my New York University post—left voluntarily, not by college or community request, should that horrid suspicion have occurred to you. I am embarrassed to confess that I have never yet been fired. I realize that this is almost as shameful as admitting to writing a history book which no pressure groups attack. It's an acknowledgment of harmlessness. I comfort myself that there is still time for redemption in the years ahead.*

A Van Til has been back to Nashville recently, however, as a reporter. At twenty, Jon Van Til, a Swarthmore College junior and a reporter for his college paper, went home again for a week to cover the sit-ins of 1960. Permit me a co-author, please, to bring us closer to date on human relations developments in a city caught up in a South-wide, indeed a nation-wide, conflict involving economic interests and moral convictions. Here is his news story from The Phoenix, April 9, 1960.

18 *Interracial Tension in Nashville*

by JON VAN TIL

A SPECTER is haunting the Southern whites in Nashville, Tennessee. It is the image of well-dressed, well-educated, well-mannered Negro college men and women sitting silently at lunch counters, coupled with the image of hundreds of white hoods in bluejeans, and with ducktails, standing behind the Negroes, jeering, mistreating, and attacking them. It is the image of law enforcement officials ignoring the actions of the whites while they arrest, and later convict, the Negroes.

Yet Nashville's schools are in the third year of a twelve-year desegregation program, and the John Kasper who sought to destroy that plan is in the Nashville workhouse. Vanderbilt University and Peabody College both admit Negro students to their graduate schools, and many community organizations boast interracial membership. Nashville's buses have been desegregated in a quiet and successful manner.

It is part of that strange code of Jim Crow that, in Nashville, Negroes may shop in department stores on equal terms with whites in all departments but one. They may try on all sorts of apparel, and it doesn't seem to hurt sales. But Negroes cannot buy their lunch at Woolworth, McClellan, Kress, Grant or Walgreen chain stores, nor at the big department stores, Harveys or Cain-Sloan, nor at any smaller white establishment. Last year a group of Negro students sought service at these counters, and met with store officials who clarified their policy—no service to Negroes on an interracial basis.

On February 13, a group of students from Nashville's Negro colleges—Fisk, Tennessee State, and American Baptist Theological Seminary—staged a non-violent sit-in at several stores. They seated themselves at lunch counters, remaining there until the counters were closed, shortly after which time they left. Further sit-ins followed, and on the 27th, violence erupted as white youngsters attacked some of the demonstrators, who did not attempt to defend themselves. Over four hundred students participated in that Saturday's sit-in, and some eighty-one were arrested for loitering and disorderly conduct. On the following Wednesday, sixty-three more demonstrators were apprehended at the Greyhound station when they refused to leave their seats at the counter despite a bomb threat that the police investigated. During both sit-ins, only non-violent demonstrators were arrested, but none of the jeering crowd behind them were.

There followed a three-week period characterized by low-level justice in the courts and community search for a solution. The eighty-one were convicted of "disorderly conduct," and at this writing are standing trial for state charges for "conspiracy to restrict trade," for which they were re-arrested. The conduct of the first trials is characterized by the students who were convicted in a single word—"farcical." The judge was repeatedly asked to recuse himself because it appeared that he had prejudged the cases.

Nashville's Mayor, Ben West, was neatly trapped between two

groups on whose support he relies, the Negroes (31 percent of Nashville's population) and what David Halberstam, a *Nashville Tennessean* reporter writing in *The Reporter*, calls the "Dixiecrat Banner" element, the reactionary group that finds its voice in the *Nashville Banner*, a paper where news rarely goes unslanted, and reporters delight in editorializing.

West has neatly juggled these groups to maintain a stranglehold on Nashville politics, but throughout March his throne was tottering, and Negroes were threatening to beat the West-backed man in a March 31 election for sheriff. So the mayor was in no mood for a divisive racial issue that might upset his tightrope balance. Results of that election, however, found his man beaten by a landslide two-to-one count, and several predominantly Negro districts went four-to-one against the mayor's machine. This election is of immense significance in Nashville politics, where Mayor West had a machine of such power he ran unopposed in the last election for mayor. If he has lost the support of the Negro people he has so long enjoyed, as it now appears, there are important changes in store on Nashville's political horizon.

Early in March, Mayor West appointed a committee to study the sit-in problem. The group consisted of two Negro college presidents, and five whites—a liberal attorney who is the head of the integrated Community Relations Conference, the head of the bar association, two businessmen, and the highly respected vice-chancellor emeritus of Vanderbilt University. To many members of the white community, this committee was the enlightened answer to the dilemma. If anyone could make sure that reason prevailed, it was the popular vice-chancellor.

To the Negroes, however, the potentiality of the committee did not seem so great. For the very constitution of the membership seemed to reflect a mistaken judgment by the whites. That the only Negroes on the committee were college presidents, one relatively new to the community, the other restricted by the fact that he is a state employee, seemed to the Negroes to indicate that the sit-ins were being treated as a student problem, not a community problem. And the Nashville Negro community strongly insists that this is much more than a temporary student craze, more than a "panty-raid type affair with a sociological twist." To the Nashville Negro, this is a movement of the bulk of the members of a race to achieve a status of equality they feel has been too long denied them. It is not stretching the term to call it a revolution, as well as a great awakening. Non-violent revolution it is, and it faces many of the same problems its violent cousin is forced to meet.

I lived in Nashville during the six years directly preceding my entrance to Swarthmore College. I returned there last week to talk with students, professors, community leaders, ministers, reporters, and other interested citizens. I found a community wrestling with an issue that apparently defies solution because it defies compromise.

To the merchants of Nashville, the issue is predominantly an economic one. They fear that the desegregation of lunch counters will lead to a loss of a significant portion of the 85-90 percent of their trade that is white—that country people will shop in surrounding towns and suburbanites will flock to the ever-growing suburban centers. A Negro economist I talked with argued differently, however. He emphasized the gains in Negro business the downtown area could anticipate if counters are desegregated, as well as the effects on Negro shopping habits continued segregation will entail. He estimated that 90 percent of the Negroes are now avoiding the downtown area—a figure some consider too high—and held that a few months of such a voluntary boycott would lead to tangible economic pressure upon the businessman. One student expressed his view by saying, "We cannot sell integration as long as we buy segregation." And behind all the arguments is the whispered fear—"We can't become a Little Rock" —for the Arkansas capital has gained no industrial plums since racial antagonism sullied its reputation in 1957.

The economic situation is thus loaded with imponderables, factors that can be best evaluated by some sort of pragmatic means like trial runs. It is subject to compromise, to experimentation. And here's the rub.

For the issue is not primarily economic to the Negro. The Negro is not just looking for a place to eat (a Negro lunch counter in Harveys failed financially); he is seeking to assert a moral right to equality that is long overdue him. A Fisk student said,

"You cannot try treating me like a human being for sixty days, and then tell me to run home if it isn't pleasant." To the Negro this is a problem of human beings, of conscience and moral right, factors that cannot be measured in economic charts and statistics.

It is central to the understanding of the sit-in movement in Nashville to realize its profound moral and spiritual nature. The inner leadership group of this movement, some twenty strong, consists of at least four ministers, one of whom, the Reverend Jim Lawson, was expelled from Vanderbilt for his association with the "civil disobedience." The ministers, working through the Nashville Christian Leadership Conference associated with Martin Luther King's group, were recognized as advisors by the students during the early stages of the sit-ins. Now, as the movement has become community-wide, the NCLC has become a full partner in leadership.

The student leaders seem to be a talented group. I sat in on one of their meetings in a church near Fisk, and was impressed by the gift of patient and lucid expression of opinion these students possessed. Quietly confident and determined, they maintain a type of high group spirit one rarely finds. And they manage to combine a high idealism fairly successfully with a sense of political reality, although not always.

That a moral issue is not subject to an economic compromise does not mean that the Negroes will not accept any reasonable plan leading to their goal—equality of consideration in lunch counter facilities. But to find such a solution is more difficult. One can hardly desegregate one seat at a time. Rev. Lawson anticipates as a tentative compromise, however, "something like opening up a controlled way with designated groups appearing at designated times." But the fundamental commitment to desegregated facilities is to the Negro an all-or-nothing moral issue. Segregated eating is as bad as none at all downtown, and non-violent resistance will continue until the day is won.

By Friday, March 25, it had been three weeks and two days since the last sit-in. Order had seemingly been restored, and community sympathy appeared to ride with the students in their quests. But by Monday, a combination of tactical weakness and remarkable coincidence was making the students appear in a more unfavorable light.

On March 2, as we have noted, the mayor's committee on sit-ins was formed. On March 3, President Wright of Fisk, a member of that committee, asked the students of Fisk to refrain from conducting demonstrations for three weeks, in order to permit the committee to reach a solution unhampered by an atmosphere of continuing tension. Since Fisk students were an important part of the group, the president's wish was honored. The period of cessation of demonstration—hardly a truce as the students withdrew completely while counters remained open, feeding shoppers for the big Nashville Extra Value Days, a sale the students could have paralyzed had they wished—this three week period ended on Thursday, March 24.

On Friday, sit-ins resumed. This time there was good police protection for the demonstrators, and only four were arrested. But equally significant was the timing of the new sit-ins. For they resumed just as the merchants were preparing a definite compromise offer to the mayor's committee, a day before it was rumored the committee was to present its report to the mayor. They resumed on the day a CBS television crew was present to film portions of a show, "Anatomy of a Demonstration." And they resumed on Friday, while Saturday was the usual day for such demonstrations to begin. Nashvillians put one, two, and three together, and shouted "fix!"

Governor Buford Ellington broke his silence on the sit-in issue to claim that CBS had rigged the sit-ins; he denounced "the most irresponsible piece of journalistic trickery I have ever heard of." The *Banner* asked if "some planning of program routine in covering a 'documentary' assignment, like lunch-counter sit-ins, was not deemed a 'technical necessity'?" Even the liberal *Tennessean*, from which Nashvillians have long expected more than hasty innuendo, raised the cry. Finding "ample cause for inquiry," an editorial claimed that having photographed meetings of the students, a "a documentary would lack the climax that naturally would follow, unless there was also a demonstration." The editorial continued, covering an exposed rear, that even if there was no advance knowledge, the mere presence of CBS might have presented "something of an opportunity" for national airing of grievances.

These verbal fireworks, coupled with sit-in resumption, gave the mayor's committee the perfect excuse for their failure to achieve the solution they were somehow to have found. Empowered with none but advisory powers, and not seen as representative by one side in the conflict, the committee had once failed to meet over an eight-day period. Now they could claim they were back "where they were," although they continued to meet and, at this writing, are reported to be near issuing a recommendation of "a significant change in the status quo at the lunch counters."

The students declared that the sit-ins were resumed because the mayor's committee could not reach a solution with the merchants. "We have no choice but to again witness in dramatic, yet loving fashion." As one minister expressed it, three weeks seemed long enough to wait for a moral decision.

As for CBS, the students denounced the rigging charges as unfounded, but the television unit was recalled from Nashville to avoid fomenting further reaction, and, after talking with the reporters and cameramen, CBS President Stanton asked for an apology from Governor Ellington. But the damage was done, and the image of the brave Negro was crowded by the new image of the Northern-led agitator.

To this reporter, it appeared as if the students' tactics were far more to blame than their ethics. They knew by Friday the nature of the merchants' "solution" then being considered—"end from end" segregation—the whites being seated from one end of the counter, the Negroes from the other. This was unacceptable to the Negroes. The students knew that the committee was nowhere near reaching an acceptable solution, and they were eager to continue their quest.

The complexity of the events of a single week in a single Southern town gives one pause when he considers the enormity of the social revolution that is at hand and the immensity of the tasks that face it. One seasoned Negro campaigner for civil rights confided to me that sometimes the struggle required for a hamburger and a cup of coffee hardly seemed worth the anxiety and discouragement it entailed. Rev. Jim Lawson spoke for the new revolution when he smiled and said, "I'm not fighting for a hamburger and a cup of coffee."

Addendum, 1961:

The report of the Mayor's committee appeared on April 5th, offering the "solution" of partial desegregation. It was rejected by both the Negro community and the merchants. A few days later the boycott of downtown stores by the Negro community went into full effect. It was not long until the merchants realized that the actual loss of Negro business was a more real danger than the potential loss of white business. Negotiating committees were established and Negro representatives and the merchants began talking together in search of a solution. As community support moved behind the Negro case with increasing strength, partially due to the bombing of a Negro attorney's home by extremists, a carefully controlled plan of desegregation was developed. On May 10 a few Negroes were served at Nashville lunch counters at prearranged times, with adequate precautions and with protection provided. Within a few weeks Negroes were being served on the same basis as anyone else; the sit-in had proved itself a potent force for social change in Nashville.   J. V. T.

VI

Bringing Up Our Children

The Background

SPEAKING of my son, Jon, reminds me. . . . The subject of my children I approach with all the hesitancy of a parent whipping out photographs of his offspring at the slightest lull in any conversation.

There are three of them—Jon, Barbara, and Roy. They have shared Bee's and my life for twenty-one, nineteen, and fifteen years respectively at this writing. Despite shared experiences, they are delightfully different, a truism parents constantly discover. Jon is a student of society and hence political science at Swarthmore. Barbara is a student of people and hence psychology at Douglass College of Rutgers. Roy is a student of the universe and hence science and mathematics in high school.

Schools are fine things and I'm all for them. But they'll never replace parents and the fun of bringing up your children.

19 *We Went to Europe as a Family*

WHEN I was young and gay, the travel bug bit me fiercely. So with Bee, my bride, off I went to Europe in the Spring. The year was 1936 and we were twenty-five. We drifted down the Moselle, the Elbe, and the Danube Rivers in our blue and silver foldboat, Long Island Duck. (Might as well remind you now that a fold-boat is the off-spring of a canoe and kayak which may be taken apart and shipped in sacks between rivers.)

Back we came the next year to travel 900 miles in Long Island Duck II. We talked·to anybody and everybody as the unblue Danube ran brown from a Black Forest toward a Black Sea. I wrote a book, *The Danube Flows Through Fascism*, a kind of hybrid of Richard Halliburton and John Gunther.

Then the travel bug bit me no more. He quietly crept away. So did the years—seventeen of them. Who stole all of those years anyway? Suddenly one cold day in 1954 I was forty-three. I don't know whether the Greeks have a word for it. But the Americans sure do. The word is not young. The word is middle-aged.

I was a college professor, well established in my chosen field. I was a suburban householder with a mortgage and a wife—same wife—whose age I have no intention of revealing to snoopers. I was par for the course as to children: Jon, fifteen; Barbara, thirteen; and Roy, nine. My insurance was high and my cash was low.

All in all, I was a respectable middle-class citizen. And the merciless travel bug chose this time to bite me fiercely again.

A humane policy of my college allied itself with the bug. Once every three full years a professor is granted a few months off with pay. His only assignment is to refresh his weary soul by drinking at whatever springs of knowledge and experience he chooses. I was due for fall 1954 and I knew what springs I needed. The Moselle. The Danube. A Long Island Duck III. Maybe a microscopic car for jogging about The Continent.

But Europe in the Fall? Europe with my family? Particularly, Europe with my three children?

Respectable middle-class families have many ties which bind. In our home the phone rings madly. Often it brings tidings of the League of Women Voters. Bee is on "the board." Otherwise, it is for Barbara, blonde and budding at thirteen, whirling in her orbit of early teen-agers all engaged in learning who they are and whence this strange new power over boys.

Jon at fifteen also had his ties. As a high school sophomore he was scheduled to begin geometry, biology, and French, and to continue English. But it was a love affair which my older son shares with Tallulah Bankhead which caused him the greatest pangs of parting. For as spring and summer wore on, the New York Giants hung grimly to first place in the National League. Jon was sometimes heard moaning, "Of all years to go to Europe —with the Giants ahead by seven games! With a World Series coming!"

Only Roy was a free man. At nine, he was as uncommitted as the weather. When he was emancipated from the fourth grade at school's end, with summer vacation and European fall lying ahead, he waved airily to his friends, "So long, boys; see you on January 3, 1955." They drooled and uttered strange cries into the soft May air.

Our best friends were as skeptical as they were tolerant. The literary among them dropped titles into their conversation: "You Can't Go Home Again," "The Revolt of the Middle-Aged Man." One bounder even suggested "Fire in the Ashes." Good souls warned us that we couldn't re-create the romantic atmosphere of Europe in the Spring, seventeen years previous. They assured us kindly that they meant that Europe had changed. But they didn't fool us even for a minute.

As to traveling with the youngest generation, Robert Benchley once contributed the definitive statement, "Traveling with children corresponds roughly to traveling third-class in Bulgaria." This is best understood by people who have traveled third-class in Bulgaria. Bee and I had.

So—the five of us decided to go to Europe in the Fall as a family.

There remained the matter of money. How much was all this going to cost, Professor, and where was the money coming from?

The same thought apparently occurred to many of our acquaintances. We would say, while trying hard to look like the sophisticated people in the travel-folders that flooded us, "We're going to Europe as a family. No, it's not a mission or a job abroad. We're just going to live in Europe a while. Just . . . live."

Glazed looks would slide over the faces of our listeners. Sometimes speculation took over. They hadn't heard news of my mother in a long time. Was she well? In fine health, never better, thank you. Had I published a textbook lately? No, I hadn't. I didn't own a Geiger counter, did I? Strike an oil well? Some people are too genteel to come right out with things.

I buried myself in guides for poor men and treatises on traveling on a shoestring. I consulted the standard travel books also, but found them too rich for my thin-blooded wallet. They advise: ". . . for unobtrusively wealthy travelers . . . where Farouk sometimes spends his nights . . . center for the international set . . . top of the heap in Venice is . . ." You feel flattered but flabbergasted.

The rock bottom figure for a family-style ocean crossing is not hard to find. One hundred and sixty-five dollars was then the cost for each person each way between New York and The Continent, tourist class, off-season, on the best of ocean liners. Children under twelve are as blessedly half-fare as on your local railroad line.

Some beg, borrow, or steal $165 times X. More thoughtful people save. Others—and here I am carefully mentioning no names —use retirement annuities in the firm but foolish conviction that they are immortal.

But there is an all-important figure that is harder to come by.

Once off the boat, how much do we spend? What is the Daily Average Per Person In Europe or, as we came to call it familiarly, DAPPIE? This is strictly an Irish Sweepstakes question. Some travel books calculate your DAPPIE anywhere from $20 to $50, transportation extra.

I consulted my crystal ball, gulped rapidly, and decided our Daily Average Per Person In Europe would be $5.50, gasoline included.

Our planning was strange and wonderful. I worked out elaborate itineraries to which we paid no attention once in Europe. Bee prepared as though for a rocket trip to the moon. Would you think of bringing to Europe—take a deep breath—a pencil sharpener, Scotch tape, flash light, extra shoe laces, a hard ball and a rubber ball, baseball hats and fielder's gloves, sneakers, moc sox, jeans, sunglasses and extra eye glasses, bathing suits, raincoats, color film, travel literature, *Huckleberry Finn*, Palgrave's *Golden Treasury*, geometry textbook, French textbook, playing cards, ball point pen and fillers, document bags, plastic shoe bags, cigarettes, flatpak tissues, Noxzema, Old Overholt, instant coffee, Suave for cowlicks, bobbie pins and curlers, money belt, Energine for spot removal, a knee supporter, sewing kit, hair clipper and scissors, iron and press cloth, five diaries, ten packs of gum and ten rolls of Life-Savers for European children as well as—time for another deep breath—aspirin, a thermometer, vitamin pills, nose drops and ear drops, S. T. 37, dramamine, and antibiotics? I wouldn't either. She did.

All of our worldly goods for August through December we packed into seven remarkable bags: a Japanese paratrooper bag, a Boy Scout duffel bag, a veteran canvas Valpak, a seventeen-year-old Yugoslavian straw bag, a worn-out brief case, a gaudy plaid shoe bag, and a sturdy item from an Army Surplus store. Porters turned pale at the sight of us. We didn't mind. We were mobile. Among the five of us we could carry all we brought to the European world. No, I don't know either how Bee got everything in.

For a hundred and fourteen days, we were to sail the seas, paddle our foldboats, jaunt by car, and live in celebrated and forgotten towns and cities across France, Austria, Germany, Switzerland, and Italy. Before we got back, each of us, save our official postcard collector, Roy, was to write thirty to forty thousand words in our personal journals concerning how the world looked to us.

First was the gray and white ocean liner, so reassuringly like a summer resort that Roy's conviction that we were doomed to sink soon vanished. He even gave up saying forebodingly, "Don't forget the Titanic."

The sports deck of the Ryndam of the Holland America Line was the magnet which drew the youngest generation. When traveling with children by ship you need not inquire whether your room location is midship nor whether the public rooms are spacious. Ask only whether the shuffleboard courts are out of the wind and available.

Three Dutch brothers became our children's partners. Roy, at nine our firmest nationalist, was at first suspicious of score keeping in a heathen tongue. The possibilities for fraud were all too obvious. For self-protection he had to learn to count in Dutch.

Paris was not only the Eiffel Tower, Arch of Triumph, Notre Dame, Napoleon's tomb and all the other tourist sights you rightly guess we visited. It was also the youngsters' introduction to the mysteries of Parisian hotels. They were fascinated by the *minuterie*, a hall light which flicks on when you press a button near the elevator, endures until you are just short of finding your keyhole, then goes off automatically leaving you in pitch darkness. They were enchanted with the pigmy elevator, a mirrored coffin which could hold three people if they were well acquainted. The elevator, passenger-operated, had a button labelled "stop." The children used it liberally for halts at such mythical levels as three and a half, three and three quarters, etcetera, on their trips between our rooms on floors two and five until a hotel employee made an impassioned address containing words not found in Jon's French textbook. Our promising scholar of French reported to me proudly, "I was able to answer '*Je ne comprends pas*'." I instructed my young in my best fatherly way, "But you shouldn't play with the *ascenseur*." Barbara asked, "Isn't the *ascenseur* the

173

man behind the desk in the lobby?" "That's the *concierge*," I responded wearily, wishing the French were sensible enough to use English. "He's cute, whatever his name is," Barbara said.

But it was the plumbing of our Paris hotel which the younger generation found most strange and exotic. Of an antique toilet with pull chain, Roy wrote indignantly, "Even Grandma's fifty-year-old plumbing works better than that." I assume he was referring to what the French would describe as the plumbing of the house of his grandmother.

Incidentally, none of the guidebooks are helpful on how to interpret French plumbing facilities to the growing mind of American youth.

In a European world where drinking water is suspect and requests for water at meals are regarded as unintelligible, what do fifteen, thirteen, and nine drink? The answer is "lemonade." In Europe "lemonade" is defined as almost anything non-alcoholic which a restaurant possesses. The journals of my children became studded with references to this peculiar beverage. "To order a lemonade is interesting. Sometimes the lemonade is like ginger ale, others orangeade, and other times like a combination of orange, lemon, grapefruit, and ginger ale." "Lemonade today with no lemons in it." "Lemonade that is sizzly and tasteless." "We had Vichy water which tasted like Alka-Seltzer." Fortunately this was not the same day on which Barbara commented, concerning some eggs, "They tasted like burned rubber on the outside and like jelly fish on the inside."

We would have needed a solid-gold shoestring if we had stayed long in Paris. So one gray morning at 5 o'clock, less than a week after we landed, a little Simca station wagon loaded with Van Tils and baggage stole from Paris. We were bound for Germany and the rivers. Yes, we bought a French car, confident that three months later we could sell if if we wished for $300 less and—let's see now—that would cost the family $3.33⅓ cents per day or 66⅔ cents Daily Average Per Person In Europe. Our Simca came to be called Marilyn, for reasons obvious at a glance.

The highway we took was the one on which the Germans had twice in my lifetime come West through France. At every crossroad there was a bearded French soldier who looked, as Bee put it, as though he were left over from World War I. Once truck loads of troops rolled toward us. "If they're Communists," said Jon, "we're the first prisoners of World War III." Barbara suggested helpfully, "Then we can go on television in 'I've Got a Secret'."

In our entire European stay, we never opened a bag at a border. Leaving France, the customs officials asked only, "Tourist?" I wasn't too quick on the uptake. Bee whispered, "Are you waiting for him to ask, 'Smugglair'?"

So after one long day—and seventeen years—we came again into Germany, the land of Dr. Jekyll and Mr. Hyde, of the honest friendly people who run amuck with militarism every second generation and take on the world. Saarburg was our destination, a lovely country town with castle ruins that look down on the Saar River, cobblestoned crooked streets, and precise patterns of grape vines that blanket the hills. In the best hotel, over one dollar dinners of rump steak, blue trout, *Wiener Schnitzel*, beer, and cokes, with three big bedrooms boasting four-foot square fluffy featherbeds, our faith in the power of our shoestring was renewed. The owner of the *Hotel zur Post* was a dignified little old lady who perpetually bowed to us as she backed out of any room. She always addressed me as Professor New York and my family swears I don't know the difference between my name and my place of birth on the long registration form one fills out at every German hotel. When the little lady presented us with a bottle of Moselle wine on our departure, we hoped that Mr. Hyde was dead and that decent Dr. Jekyll had come back home to Germany to stay.

We bought two foldboats at a sports store in Trier, one a vivid red and silver and the other a blue and silver descendant of earlier Long Island Ducks. ("Stop worrying, dear; we can sell both of them at a profit in America.") We left our car at the local canoe club. For nine blissful days we drifted and paddled 112 miles down the Moselle River to the Rhine.

To describe foldboating to one who has never cruised on a European river is hopeless. It's lolling deliciously in the sun in the fond belief that a paddle is something to lean on. It's waving to peasants on the steep shale slopes of the vineyards. It's riding the rips that flash around stone jetties that narrow the river and speed its current; it's whirling into backwaters and spinning out again into the main stream.

At noon we landed in little towns and stretched our legs in market squares that looked like the backdrops for Shakespearean plays. Each evening we found rooms for the night in a local river front hotel. Our boats we left overnight in places as various as a river bank, a dark cellar, a grand ballroom of a hotel, and a giant jail of a boat house under a bridge. After dinner we often climbed to the inevitable ruined castle brooding over the town. (Barbara once found it diary-worthy that "Today we passed a town with a *whole* castle.")

And sometimes, truth being truth, we noticed the little spots on the river, as Jon put it, and we grimly sat it out, covered by raincoats or whatever, until rain, the arch enemy of the river man, moved on to new conquests. Then there was the matter of our landing places. Jon holds that the old Captain was not at his best here. "One thing must be understood. Dad has a good eye for picking the dirtiest, slimiest, most mucky, icky, gooey spots in which to dock." Removing river ooze from under her toenails one night, Bee said briefly, "Sometimes I wonder." I always claim it's the unexpected which lies around the corner that gives life its tang.

Sometimes age and youth saw things differently. Bee and I are devotees of Beilstein on the Moselle but the youngest generation rejects its memory. Beilstein is a lovely undiscovered village crammed into a cleft that climbs a hill. The great old fort-like houses have heavy rock bases and their lowest windows are fifteen feet up. The newer houses have doors casually dated 1714 or 1758 over beautiful brass knockers in the form of fists. The old town rises steeply from the Moselle's edge to a church with a black Madonna which towers over the town and graciously overlooks the goings-on below. For Beilstein's convivial citizenry and visitors walk continuously though unsteadily across the crazily slanting cobblestone square from the Alte Wine House, to the Burg Metternich Tavern, to whatever that pink *gasthaus* is called, and then to the Felsenkeller, or Stone Cellar, where we found the only available lodging in town on a Saturday night.

On our night in town, all of Beilstein appeared to assemble in our one-room wine cellar with flood-lit back wall of sheer rock. German people happen to sing roaring songs over their Moselle wine. Just above the Stone Cellar were the two rooms where we presumably "slept."

Beilstein went into the black books of the children. While I was reflecting mellowly that the tourists frantically shuffle up and down the Rhine looking for the Middle Ages while all the while yesterday is at Beilstein, Barbara was writing "Got an awful hotel with the only two rooms in the place over a wine bar sleeping on four beds for five people. Horrible. Beilstein." I guess it must depend upon your point of view.

Where the Moselle met the Rhine, we packed the foldboats. Marilyn was driven to us by an employee of the sports store where we bought our boats. The cost was his rail fare home plus a tip. We tied the foldboat sacks on top of the car and headed south. For the nine-day cruise on the Moselle, our Daily Average Per Person In Europe was $3.35.

In the Black Forest, cuckoo clock madness overcame us. Roy recorded, "We saw a cuckoo clock shop and then it started." How can madness be avoided when Black Forest clocks sell for ninety-six cents up? When the delirium had passed, we had added to our baggage eight clocks, elaborately carved, surmounted by proud birds, and telling the hour at the slightest provocation.

We might have stayed forever hiking in the Black Forest or foldboating on Lake Constance to a reconstructed Stone Age village and to an island with tropical vegetation in the shadow of the frozen Alps. But the Danube still ran. So we came back to our brown river and a brush with the Angel of Death. But not on the old growler, which we found in flood. The brush came nearby in a little walled town with clock towers dating from 1200 over each of its three entrances. Kelheim, beside the German Danube, was our low point. There Roy, our youngest and strongest, came down with pain.

It is a desolate feeling to be alone in a foreign land with a sick child whose illness the local doctor cannot diagnose. Nothing helps—medicine, time, reading *Huckleberry Finn* aloud, planning ahead. For stabbing hours you try to turn back the irreversible past and look into the unknowable future. When your child jolts in a Red Cross ambulance to the hospital in the nearest city and three deadly-serious quiet doctors tell you they are not sure but they will have to cut in at once to look—their words are "exploratory operation"—you are trapped in the dead end of your emotions. Now everything depends on the foreign-tongued people, your late enemies. As they get ready to take your youngest to the operating room, he says to you only "Go with me as far as you can" and all the lights of your life seem to go out inside you.

An orderly comes in and carefully carries the wasted body to the operating room. You say to your wife, "Now you can cry." After the crying is done, you can only wait and try to persuade yourself that your world couldn't possibly end this way. Other people maybe. Not you. Ages later the stretcher goes by with its silent cargo. Appendicitis with peritonitis. Peritonitis means only one thing to you.

Now times becomes eternity. Then the doctors come out and you see in their eyes a look you know well. It's the look of the professional who has done a difficult job, a look that says no one else knows what we've done or how well we did it, but we know and that's enough. Then you know it's only a matter of waiting for him to be well.

During the eighteen days of waiting, either Bee or I stayed with Roy every day and almost every night. While he played with tiny European model automobiles, family trios ventured out on side trips. So some of us saw Munich rebuilding. Some walked on the great rubble pile called Nuremberg and some went back to the Middle Ages at Dinkelsbühl and Rothenburg, towns out of the fairy tales. Once Jon and Barbara paddled placidly below a castle at Reidenburg where German generals awaited the Nuremberg trials and where refugees from communism now live. The quiet Altmühl Canal presented no problems to Captain Jon after his day of navigation with me along a stretch of the flooding Danube that squirms tortuously through the high chalk cliffs.

Naturally, we came to know best our hospital city. In Regensburg we saw most clearly the strange mixture that is modern Germany. Today and yesterday are side by side in this city of 108,000 population. There are juke boxes, orange juice, *The Glenn Miller Story* with long German sentences spilling harshly and peculiarly from Jimmy Stewart's lips, the German-American Women's Club sponsoring that great international common denominator called Bingo, *Amerika Haus* with a magnificent library of American books and magazines, the Iron Curtain forty miles away, an escalator in one of the department stores, slot machines, modern furniture, jazz, Gillettes, and—I am happy to add —penicillin. The new world sits oddly on Regensburg with a Roman gate built in the time of Marcus Aurelius, a bridge with great arches through which the Danube has hurtled since the 1100's, a *Rathaus* with medieval torture instruments in the basement, a smoky little wurst kitchen regularly flooded out yet persisting since the eleventh century, a great Catholic cathedral two blocks from Martin Luther Street, and an imperturbably neutral Danube charging like a maddened elephant in a hurry to get to the Black Sea.

In Regensburg in a Germany which balances between East and West, there are two large signs painted on flame red backgrounds. They are almost opposite each other on Maximilian Strasse. One, on an old building, says, "Communist Party Headquarters." The other, on a fence around an excavation, says "F. W. Woolworth's —to be opened soon." Personally, I'm betting on Woolworth's.

With the Simca station wagon converted into a semi-ambulance in which Roy might stretch out, off we went on a great four-lane highway called the *Autobahn*, off to Austria—to ice cream sodas, hamburgers, hot water, American newspapers, broadcasts, and movies! For in Austria there was a little piece of America called an Army installation where a young niece of ours, her lieutenant husband, and their babies lived. We stayed in a guest house nearby. Roy began running up mountain sides again.

Once we crawled by Simca up Austria's highest mountain, Gross Glockner, a few days before the road was abandoned for the winter to the unstoppable snow drifts. Marilyn toiled in the second of her four forward speeds as the road twined around twenty-five hairpin turns and through tunnels amid an infinite loneliness of ice and snow on top of the world. Roy, a veteran of Colorado's Trail Ridge Road and Mount Evans, looked at the great desert of snow in a land of nobody and nothing and asked, "Don't you think they're overdoing it?"

The cold came on and we fled further south. On the day we crossed Switzerland's Saint Gothard Pass to the new vegetation, architecture, and people of the Mediterranean world, Jon, a tolerant fifteen, wrote, "I have come to know the German language and have come to know the three types of German people, all very different. The Germans doubtful of their former enemies, the simple Austrians, and the modern Swiss. I seem to catch the liking of these people."

I sometimes wonder if Roy, at nine, ever quite caught "the liking of these people." Germanic or Mediterranean, they deviated from America's way, especially as to sanitation, and he disapproved. Thinking about the hospital, he said, "They kept scrubbing the floors all the time. But they didn't change my sheets and they didn't swat the flies. Don't they understand about germs?" Of Italy, he asked, "How long have these people been in business?" I tried to tell him. "Why don't they build more bathrooms instead of so many churches?" These are hard questions for nine to answer—or even forty-three. Whenever we talked about the noticeable Americanization of Europe, Roy had one comment, "Good."

The days grew shorter in mid-November but we put a foldboat together again for a week on Lake Como. Home base was a little pension intimately inhabited by a father, mother, old grandmother, and little Marialena, exactly Barbara's age. Marialena was learning English in school through stilted little sentences and we traded vocabularies. The two thirteen-year-old girls later corresponded and traded photographs.

Eventually we packed Long Island Duck III and hit the tourist trail, the eternal triangle across the top of Italy to Milan and Venice, down to Rome, and up to the Italian Riviera. We might be tourists from now on, rather than foldboat vagrants, but we were going to pick and choose foldboat-style. So, in Milan we had a single purpose—to see *The Last Supper*. Barbara wrote, "A single long white room—at one end a complicated picture of the crucifixion and at the other end *The Last Supper* by Leonardo da Vinci. . . In 1945 the whole building but the two walls where the paintings are were ruined by bombs. What detail. Almost three dimensional. I tried to grasp the fact that I was standing in front of the 500-year-old painting right where it was painted by a man who knew everything. Engineer, architect, astronomer, politician, sculpturer, and artist. Jesus accepting the fact that he must die, but the Apostles trying to figure out how they can save their King. The hands and the faces in such detail. This is religion alive. I could have spent hours looking at this piece of art, never equaled. The beauty beyond words. 500 years old. Judas sitting forward, while Peter and John whisper. Each face different and beautiful. A real experience never to be forgotten."

Of course we fell desperately in love with Venice with its great Square of St. Marks, its aggressive pigeons who steal corn from your pockets, its gondoliers who handle their bulky crafts with skill that excites the admiration of any river man. We devoured Rome—one day in the Forum and Colosseum, another in St. Peter's and the Sistine Chapel, another out in the countryside traveling the Appian Way and visiting the catacombs. Yes, I know we should have stayed a year.

Barbara fluttered a rash of postcards home after an encounter in the Vatican museum. "Jon saw a postcard of the statue of the Discus Thrower which we tried to find. No luck. But as we were walking down the hall we saw a man passing us who looked very familiar. It was Charlton Heston, the famous movie star, dressed in a gray seedy tweed suit. I should have asked him for his autograph but he was soon gone. We then found the original statue of the Discus Thrower which was very, very good. But I prefer Charlton Heston any day."

How else to close our trip but with the Sunny Riviera? We chose the Italian Riviera. We knew exactly what we wanted for our last nine days in Europe—an azure cove with villa-speckled hills rising from the water, a tiny town of a dozen buildings, a hotel on the lake side of the road if you please, rooms looking out to the sea and the sun, and, since beauty is inedible, magnificent Italian cooking in addition. Naturally all at a low price. But there is nothing like that at Rapallo or at Santa Marghuerita either and we were within a mile of the end of a little hook jutting into the Mediterranean.

We rounded almost the last curve. The vision was there. Cove, town, hotel. A balcony overlooking a beach on the Mediterranean. Three rooms opening on the balcony. A mile from the fishing village and yacht harbor of Portofino. Rooms and all meals, including breakfasts on the balcony, for $5.27 each person each day. We were the sole guests and were magnificently served by a cook, a waiter, and a manager. The owning family paid little heed to us or to the wine-dark sea; they had just gotten a television set.

Should I tell you the name of the place and ruin my chances for staying there when I come to Europe in the Winter seventeen years from now? I might as well. Seventeen years is a long time. The hotel at Paraggi. I guess it means Paradise. P.S.: In accordance with Emerson's Law of Compensation, it rained abundantly on the Sunny Riviera. But we read *The Sea Around Us* and *The Golden Treasury* at the fireplace, paddled a foldboat, hiked along the sea, and swam luxuriously in the Mediterranean on December third.

We chose a ten day return trip which contained a Mediterranean cruise in the bargain. We embarked at Genoa, sailed west to Cannes, then southeast to Naples, thence to Gibraltar and through the Azores. I wanted to take a ship that stopped at Halifax too, but then I never have known what enough means.

On the high seas, the father of the family spent some hours with pencil and paper. Later, he proclaimed some figures. The Daily Average Per Person In Europe was $4.77.

Our DAPPIE included all food, clothing, shelter, hospital and medical costs. (Blessings on you, Red Cross, for the ambulance. Thank you, Blue Cross, for the hospital insurance. From now on, you will be two crosses we will be happy to bear.) Our Daily Average Per Person In Europe included gas and maintenance for Marilyn, shipping the foldboats by rail across the Alps, phony lemonade and gourmet's wine, a stream of tips, riotous living and heaven knows what all. The works. Also included was our loot: eight Black Forest clocks, three Swiss watches, two Austrian leather brief cases, four paintings, a rosary from Rome for one Grandma and hand-embroidered Italian linen cloth for the other, a score of little gifts such as Hummel figurines for friends and relatives, and an abundance of souvenirs, including Jon's pennants and wood-pictures, Roy's miniature cars and planes, and Barbara's glass menagerie.

Naturally, DAPPIE did not include what we brought with us to Europe in the seven remarkable bags, nor ocean transport, nor foldboats saleable at a profit. Nor did it include an immigrant, Marilyn. To buy, equip, document, insure, and ship her home, cost two thousand one hundred dollars. In place of our venerable 100,000 mile Pontiac, now Marilyn daily ran the roads at 27 miles to a gallon and parked in places where nothing else fits.

But no one cared any longer about the DAPPIE, and no one listened to the poor man tell the average for each nation: France $7.52, Germany $3.89, Austria $4.07, Switzerland $8.86, and Italy $5.53. We had been to Europe, hadn't we? Who cared what it cost?

You know what people say when they come home, "Being away was wonderful. Now it's great to be home." So you know how we felt when we sailed into New York harbor. Jon put it with starry-eyed sincerity on the inside back cover of the only space remaining in volume 2 of his 40,000-word journal. "We are in New York, America. We have found out that there is no country in the world like America. I believe that we must continue to help the European nations. It has been a great wonderful experience and I'm certain I shall return to Europe. I shall never forget Fall, 1954." Roy said, "When we passed the Statue of Liberty on our way to Europe you said I would look at it different the next time I saw it again. I didn't know what you were talking about then. But now I do."

Then we slipped back into the life of Suburbia. The phone rang madly again. It was the League of Women Voters for Bee and the First Teeners' Club for Barbara. Jon worried about the Giants. Roy built menacing model airplanes, probably as protection against foreign people who spit in the streets and don't wash their hands after going to the bathroom.

The three children went back to school again, and made the same grades they used to make. Barbara mined her journal for the fifty words she misspelled abroad and made these her spelling list for the first two weeks of school. The industrious ant of the family, Jon, having carried his textbooks abroad, moved back smoothly into his high school classes. I like his understatement, "It isn't easy to learn geometry by yourself while traveling in Europe." The fiddling grasshopper of the family, Roy, looked at me solemnly while going to bed on the night of January 2, 1955. He said: "Dad, an awful thing has happened. I've forgotten how to divide and multiply. And that's what school is all about." It took the whole evening of January 3 to bring him up to the level of his classmates.

Though our middle-class responsibilities swallowed us up again, we had our memories.

Anybody else in this family besides me want to go see the rest of the world sometime?

Ever look intently at a child's room? After you get over being appalled, try the geological approach to accumulated layers of interests suggested here. You may discover an emerging personality, some life trends. I did as I sat in the room of my youngest on his twelfth birthday and set down some observations for Childhood Education.

20 *Of Protons, Planes and Presley*

TODAY is Lincoln's Birthday, 1957. It is also Roy's birthday. The youngest of our brood has reached the age of twelve.

Once we had three small children. Now we have a seventeen-year-old young man, a fifteen-year-old young woman and Roy. Come with us to his room. You will see what occupies his out-of-school hours.

Roy's room is small and square and simple. It contains only four pieces of furniture: bed, table, bookcase, and combination desk-dresser with formica top. Basically, this room is like millions of boys' bedrooms.

Yet when you enter Roy's room, you know at once who lives there. Roy, Eleven just reached Twelve, lives there.

Models of deadly war planes hang from the ceiling, poised to blast one into oblivion. On a bulletin board of wallboard, newly cut and age-yellowed clippings elbow each other for living room. Baseball gloves, tennis rackets and a basketball occupy a corner; Roy plays guard for the Junior High. Encyclopedias opened to the letter "S" are stacked on the desk, making detailed maps of South America being the passion this week. A painstakingly drawn chart of the structure of protons, neutrons and electrons in twenty-four elements hangs on the wall. A stack of 45 rpm records tilts crazily, held in balance by a music store list of the top forty songs of the week and a hat labeled "Elvis." In this museum one looks a long while before one notices the bed, the table, the bookshelves, and the desk-dresser.

Can we uncover Seven among these remembrances of things past? Or has Seven joined One through Six, lost residues of past ages washed by changing times into the attic, the dark corners of closets and the hands of younger children of our friends? The quest culminates in an abandoned and unhonored cigar box on the lowest shelf of the bookcase. The box is full of rocks. Let adults have their photograph albums; at Seven, Roy's souvenirs of travel were rocks. Crystals tell of Mammoth Cave, Kentucky; geodes and mica testify to the existence of the Colorado Rockies; petrified wood recalls Arizona; coquina, the ancient Spanish fort at St. Augustine; garnets, an aunt's farm in Connecticut.

Seven was also when Roy discovered the universe, spurred by older brother Jon's enthusiasm for astronomy. Among the rubble are star maps and a telescope and a shoe box into which one peers at black paper pricked with pin points, luminous constellations when held against a light.

Astronomy persisted through Eight and even has some survival value today. But at Nine, the great outdoors entered the room— fortunately in the form of leaves rather than entire trees and live animals. The leaves, now tired and worn at the edges, were picked from every field within bicycle range. Some are unfamiliar to local botanists because at Nine Roy traveled through Europe with his family by canoe and car. Let Jon have his pennants of European cities and countries mounted on burlap along a wall of his room. Let Barbara have her glass menagerie of figurines, animals, vases and tiny dolls. Roy has his leaves from such exotic settings as an island with tropical vegetation, believe it or not, in the shadow of the snow-capped Alps.

Home again in America, Ten constructed model planes in every waking hour outside of school. The formica desk-dresser top was cleared of competitive debris. The room often smelled of glue. Since the pieces which make up modern plane models are myriad, precision akin to the watchmaker's was developed. Accumulated savings from earlier allowances went into Sabrejets, Thunderstreaks, Zeros, and Spitfires. Today, as they swoop across the room on strings reaching from wall to wall, the dust gently descends on them. But at night Roy can look at them as he lies in bed and pats Wags, asleep on the floor. Perhaps in our perilous world, ever poised on the brink of imminent catastrophe, this is protection of a sort.

In Roy's school experience, there have been vast patches of desert in which he routinely learned his subjects and obediently went through the paces, while life and education began at three-thirty and continued through week ends. But last spring, through a perceptive sixth-grade teacher, he discovered electricity. For a Science Fair in the classroom he built a battery-operated quiz game which obligingly lights up when you touch a pointer to the right answer. Electricity led into a collection of chemicals, including arsenic and cyanide, viewed with alarm by his parents.

But poisons are trivial compared to a lethal discovery of late Eleven. Roy entered into the celestial harmonies of the spheres—by way of Elvis Presley. He spent hours with his radio until he had tape-recorded every one of Elvis' records. If called on today for an impromptu recital, his parents no doubt would faultlessly render "Hound Dog" and "Don't Be Cruel." But, as Ecclesiastes consolingly pointed out, this too will pass away.

Map-making is coming over the horizon. For his birthday, Roy has asked not only for a new album, "Strictly Elvis," but also for a first-rate atlas. He has been studying the comparative virtues of Rand McNally versus Hammond. There are murmurings of compiling a book of facts, charts and maps on Asia with a collaborator. He estimates it may run three hundred pages.

What will jostle the planes, the telescope, the chart, the chemicals, the records and the growing "smorgasbord" of books if Roy becomes an Orientalist, we cannot predict. But we are confident that another layer will be added to the archaeology and personality of Roy's room . . . and Roy.

VII
*Participating
in the
Great Debate*

The Background

In the nineteen sixties we live in a time of the Great Debate on American education. This is as it should be. The danger to good education lies not in vigorous and informed debate but in apathy, indifference, and neglect.

Contrary to a propagated stereotype, professional educators in school systems and colleges have long been urging public participation in the Great Debate. Many are the citizens' groups on education which owe their origin to professional initiative and encouragement.

If anything, the professionals in elementary and secondary education have leaned over backward in avoiding important roles in the Great Debate. They have come perilously close to abdicating their responsibility for speaking out on current controversial issues. Yet as experienced schoolmen who are dedicating their lives to educational theory and application, they too should have a significant part in discussion which precedes decision.

Among the participants in the debate are the academic critics of modern education. They call for "tough" programs with a moratorium on "frills." Many want to get back to something vaguely described as "the good old days"—whenever that was.

The public didn't pay too much attention until Sputnik soared in 1957. Then, amid the attendant hysteria, some of the extremists among the academic critics captured the public's ear and eye via the mass media, and the root of all evil was traced to Miss Jones who teaches the seventh grade in your town and who was purportedly seduced by a conspiracy of the villainous "educationists."

I have some convictions about these matters. Such beliefs have found their way into the essays which follow on communication, curriculum improvement, discipline, delinquency, gifted children, history teaching, group dynamics, and the meaning of today's social and cultural developments for the school program.

§ Well before the late 1950's when the academic critics flailed away at modern education, it was clear that the profession of education was failing to communicate to the people through the popular journals and other mass media. A recent raise in dues has enabled the National Education Association to expand its communication activities. Yet a condition of "too late and too little" still persists as to communication concerning modern schools. Let's Communicate Democratic Education *is a plea for educational popularization.*

21 *Let's Communicate Democratic Education*

SAID *Time*, speaking of educators meeting in convention, "Unfortunately, much of their talk would be meaningless to nonprofessional ears. At a time when United States education had extended its mission to embrace more lives and for a longer time than ever before, it had paradoxically moved farther and farther away from the public grasp."

Whether you applauded or deplored some of the copy, the validity of this quotation deserves acknowledgment. *Time* may well cry *touché*, as did the James Thurber fencer on cleanly slicing off his opponent's head.

We need translation by American educators. It is absurd to use the elaborate apparatus of American education—its theories, research, teacher-training, personnel—to produce good educational experiences for children and youth, only to sit by passively as these experiences are misinterpreted by minorities within communities. It is absurd for a profession to invest substantial time and money in Thirty School studies, in evaluative summaries and surveys which answer many public doubts, only to allow these to remain the exclusive property of graduate students, locked from the general public.

It would be different if educational ideas were not translatable. But they are. Certainly they are more understandable than scientific ideas which draw on complex mathematical and physical data. Yet what a laudable job has been done in communicating scientific developments to the public!

Under the elaborate verbiage of modern education are horse sense ideas. Under the sonorous research titles are the verifications of many of these horse sense ideas. Ideas like studying problems that are important to young people's lives. Learning the 3 R's better through having a purpose. Helping youth get ready for a vocation. The value of varied interests and hobbies. Learning democracy by living democratically. Learning at different speeds because no two people are exactly alike. A good education for those not going to college as well as for those planning college entrance.

The pragmatic American people are fond of horse sense. They support what seems reasonable to them. They are willing to have the schools make sense. Some studies even seem to indicate that the public—not the noisy little minorities—may be more pragmatic about education than the educators!

Let's translate. Let's take the public into our confidence. Modern education has the better arguments and the evidence to back them up.

Let's not fall into the trap of defensively refuting libels. "We do so teach the 3 R's!" The libels stay in the public mind. The refutations are often forgotten.

If I were an education dean—a fate which merciful providence has happily spared me—I'd hire me a few potential Stuart Chases. I'd instruct these professors of popularization to resist the seductions of original research and the further refinement of theory which engaged almost everybody else on the faculty. I'd tell them that their tenure depended on their ability to speak United States about education over television and in film shorts and to write United States about education for the popular magazines and press. They might even look forward to full professorships of popularization when they wrote the Book of the Month!

If I were a superintendent who saw beyond his city limits, I'd communicate the forward-looking practices of my school system not only to my own PTA and local newspaper. Public opinion in the local community largely depends on the opinion-shaping nation-wide mass media. A free-lance journalist might collaborate with me on a magazine article. A radio or television station might carry into many homes the discussions of a panel of teenagers from my high school. A documentary film of good practices might pay for itself.

If I were a foundation—it would be an interesting feeling to be a foundation, wouldn't it?—I'd found a magazine on education for the lay public. There are magazines for the general public on hosts of matters—religion, science, sports, mechanics, politics, needlework, intercultural relations, and model railroad building. But where is the popular magazine on education for John Q. Public who isn't a PTA officer or a school board official? My magazine, *American Education*, might be pocket-size, but it would not be a reprint affair. Instead, it would contain skillful popularizations by educational journalists like the members of the Educational Writers Association and by those educators not yet entirely corrupted by academese, pedaguese, and gobbledygook. Plenty of pictures. Case studies. Profiles of the nobler Romans among us. Maybe even some of the jokes told at convention at Chicago and Atlantic City—but not all.

If I were an executive secretary of an educational organization, I'd never hold a convention in an American city without sponsoring at least one meeting especially for the public. I'd go all out with the newspapers and the school system to get a good audience for my most intelligible members and to get press coverage for the conventions. Back in the home office, leads for good stories and scripts on modern educational developments might be fed systematically to journalists, radio stations, aspiring writers, TV producers.

If I were a professor of education—but wait—I *am* a professor of education. Can this heretical doctrine apply to me too? Must even a professor communicate through such vulgar media as popular magazines, press, radio, rather than exclusively through monographs, yearbooks, and the "little magazines" of education? Give me a bit more time and I feel confident that I shall work out an adequate rationalization, exempting me. Even as you, dear reader?

I still think that the matter of who participates in curriculum improvement is not as simple as it might appear. The question "who decides what" is particularly complicated. I know that the standard cliché of the educational liberal is to the effect that since the schools belong to the people, the people can and should do exactly as they see fit. But I fear that a new generation of school administrators has accepted the cliché as a justification for abdication from educational leadership.

You may call me a modern educator. But I am sufficiently old-fashioned to believe with Thoreau and Emerson in the importance of the individual and the value of leadership.

22 *Curriculum Improvement:*
Who Participates?

Who should participate in improving the curriculum? To the modern democratic educator, the answer does not seem to be difficult. All who are affected should participate. Parents and other members of the lay public, teachers and administrators, children and youth. So it seems that our question is answered.

But if the answer is as easy as this, why isn't the curriculum everywhere throughout the nation improved through the participation of all affected? What should be done everywhere seems clear enough. Follow the principles of good group process. Have everybody in for study and agreement. Carry out the mandate of all. Selah!—the result is curriculum change supported by everyone.

This happens mostly in Fairyland. Why?

Successful group work is a difficult business. Many group members have difficulty in accepting and even more difficulty in living by the basic principles of group process. Stuart Chase summarized these principles well in *Roads to Agreement*. Successful agreement involves genuine participation with everyone getting into the act. It involves the release of group energy into constructive channels. It involves clear communication among all and a mutual understanding of semantics and logical traps. It involves willingness to consider the facts first, as in the scientific method, despite thirst for theoretical controversy. It involves the participants' feeling secure while afloat on the risky seas of group consideration.

The people who must come to accept and live by such principles, if agreement is to be achieved, come from highly varied economic, social, religious, and political backgrounds in an age of anxiety and in a culture in conflict. They perceive each other quite differently. Their personality patterns are deeply set.

Impossible, then, to achieve roads to agreement? Not at all. As American folk-say puts it, in this country the impossible just takes a little longer to achieve. Not impossible. But not easy either. Not to be exorcised by the voodooism of a single sociodrama at the opening of a conference, useful as sociodrama is.

If all who are affected should take part, everyone in the school community should be in on the improvement program. Here's a tough one too. Everyone is quite a few people, even in Crossroads, U.S.A., as well as in a Los Angeles or New York City area surrounding a school. If we settle for representatives, there is a problem of proper balance among groups. If we settle for samples, there is a problem of achieving a fair sample. Granted that fair representation can be achieved, many who are affected will be left out. Without personal participation in planning, they may feel uninvolved and may regard their representation as merely nominal.

But assume we can get fair representation in planning sessions and, through ingenuity in reporting back and through use of instruments, some involvement of many others in a more distant and less personal relationship. Assume planning sessions use group processes skillfully. Many agreements and shared actions will result. But agreement by all on everything is unlikely in as diverse a society as America.

Should total agreement be insisted upon as a prerequisite to action? Though the democratic and peaceable Quakers answer yes, some students of group action fear that the price of total agreement may be too high. The price may be long periods of inaction while the disagreement waits in the freezer, cooling off. Or the disagreement may be irreconcilable, as a democrat's difference in ideology from the authoritarianism called communism. Or the price may be obfuscation of real differences, specious agreement on generalities, with "operators" then free to interpret supposed consensus as they will. Therefore some regard total agreement as strictly for the totalitarians.

The knottiest problem of all may be the proper responsibilities and relationships of those who make up "all who are affected." Specifically, what are the responsibilities and relationships of the professionals and the public? Who decides what? Discussion of this is usually between those who compare education to medicine and those who say that education should follow public mandates.

Those who use the medical analogy argue that educators, like doctors, must diagnose and treat rather than have laymen prescribe, else what avail the careful training and practical experience of the specialist? Those who urge following popular mandates say that since the schools belong to the people, educators should assume leadership yet always recognize that decision-making in education, all the way from broad policy-making to decisions on technical details of teaching, such as phonics, belongs to the people. This latter position usually includes a democratic faith that the people will study the facts, will support full and free inquiry, and will judge well.

But another dimension should enter this discussion of responsibilities and relationships of the professionals and the public. The attempts to capture man's mind through capturing his children's schools never cease. Suppose the people of community X—not a minority but whatever you usually mean when you say the people —decide to reject free inquiry. Suppose the people of community X want indoctrination of a set of not-to-be-examined but claimed-to-be-good answers on certain economic, social, religious, or political issues. Yet the educators in school leadership positions in community X believe that there can be no freedom without freedom of the mind and consequently support the method of intelligence. The people of community X reject freedom of inquiry.

The educational leadership of community X regards freedom of inquiry as fundamental. What, then, is the modern democratic educator's highest loyalty? What should a man do? (Or, reversing the question, suppose the educational leadership of community X, not the people, rejects free inquiry and sponsors some claimed-to-be-good impositions?). . .

The easy answer, "All who are affected should participate," remains valid. But it doesn't answer some related problems.

Writing for the NEA Journal is always a challenge. That circulation! During the late nineteen fifties, it was more than 700,000. If potential readership were not enough to put a writer on his mettle, there is also the cold fact of strict space limitations. What can one say about discipline in a few hundred words? Here is what I managed to say in 800 words in Better Curriculum—Better Discipline. *(What's the dash for? To save space, naturally.)*

23 *Better Curriculum— Better Discipline*

MAINTAINING discipline is the Nemesis of the inexperienced teacher. Since Nemesis visits with retribution any violation of the natural equilibrium, I suspected that she might scourge me with discipline problems when I came out of college poorly prepared for teaching—loaded with content but ignorant of both youth and my craft.

Yet the only teaching job I could find in the lean days of the Great Depression was in a reform school which had no books, no pencils, no paper, no chalk, no course of study, no *nothing!* All the school had was delinquents from New York City's slums. It had plenty of those.

When, in a barren classroom, I first faced 30 teenage delinquents, I felt like a character in a Kafka nightmare. I saw before me boys who were sullen or mocking or hostile. As to discipline, the choice presented me seemed stark. Either I must put into these delinquents the fear of the master—namely me—through every scrap of authority I could muster, including a coercive curriculum, or I must work jointly with them to develop a curriculum somehow related to their lives. I gambled on the latter course. As poet Robert Frost put it, in "The Road Not Taken,"

> Two roads diverged in a wood, and I—
> I took the one less traveled by,
> And that has made all the difference.

For me, it has been a good road, the less traveled way of achieving discipline through developing a curriculum relevant to learners.

Year after year, the battle about discipline has gone on between those who advocate physical punishment, sarcasm, strictness, and those who advocate the approach of love, acceptance, permissiveness. In the verbal exchanges, the latter approach is gaining ground.

Yet, as the interminable battle goes on, I have the uneasy feeling that the importance of a curriculum which makes sense is too often unmentioned. This is a grave oversight, because the child, the potential candidate for either the harsh or the permissive treatment, is a youngster whose behavior is caused. And an important part of the casual environment is the curriculum we educators choose.

Let's face it. Again and again, our school discipline problems grow out of a curriculum which does not make sense to the learner. A class in which academic content bears no relationship to the needs or the world of the learner is a breeding place for rebellious disturbances.

The thing that is wrong and trouble-causing, we often hear, is that the content is "too hard" or, less frequently, "too easy." But "too hard" and "too easy" assume that the curriculum content and method are fundamentally right, and only the level on which the instruction is pitched is wrong.

All too often, this assumption is fallacious. When the curriculum itself is trivial, pedantic, unrelated to the learner's needs, irrelevant to the social realities which surround him, the question of level is of little importance. The real villain is often the curriculum itself, not the level.

The importance of a meaningful curriculum is documented as occasional educators sponsor formal or informal research on discipline. After a continuing informal study of discipline was made by his faculty, the principal of a junior high school in Morris Plains, New Jersey, reported, "The number of discipline referrals to the office ebbs and flows according to the kind of job an individual teacher does in planning, motivating, and presenting the period's work."

Thirty-eight practices associated with effective discipline were tested through observation of Baltimore teachers. Conclusions were:

"The practice of using all available equipment and visual aids to embellish and enrich a lesson so as to interest and promote the learning growth of pupils is closely associated with effective discipline. . . The practice of presenting the subject matter in a vital and enthusiastic manner, of making the subject matter appealing so that . . . it acts as a check or control to incipient misbehavior, is closely associated with effective discipline."

Better discipline will prevail when learning experiences relate closely to the present interests and needs of children who see the use of what they are learning. Better discipline will prevail when learning is related to the social realities which surround the child. Better discipline will prevail when we practice what we preach as to respect for personality. Better discipline will prevail as we develop active student participation, creative contributions, social travel, and all else that fosters significant experiences. Better discipline will grow out of a better curriculum in a better society.

You may know a little Jimmy who is a discipline problem despite an apparently meaningful curriculum. So do I. But in our concern for unconforming little Jimmy, let us not neglect improving the environment of millions of Jimmys through gearing our curriculum to the lives of the young and avoiding needless disciplinary struggles.

ᐱᔥ Combating Juvenile Delinquency Through Schools *was pre-pared under unusual circumstances. The article is essentially the testimony I submitted to a hearing conducted by the Subcommittee to Investigate Juvenile Delinquency, the United States Senate, in the summer of 1955.*

What a host of viewpoints came before this honestly conducted hearing! With characteristic interest and courtesy, Senator Estes Kefauver of Tennessee listened to all of us. I fear my testimony was not as glamorous as that of either the "get tough" spokesmen or the monomaniacs who know the only possible answer. I make only a modest claim for my advocacy of good modern schools to combat delinquency—it's more sensible.

24 *Combating Juvenile Delinquency Through Schools*

WITH the rise in juvenile delinquency, the medicine men are once again prescribing their favorite panacea. For prevention and cure of delinquency, we are advised to "get tough," "go back to the woodshed," "apply the nightstick." A feature article urges, "Let's Get Tough with Delinquents." A religious personality tells his television audience that juvenile delinquency has increased in direct ratio to the decline of razor strops and woodsheds. A letter to the *New York Times* from a former official of the Department of Correction of New York City states "that the presence and application of the night stick by police against young hoodlums will act as a deterrent to delinquency." A metropolitan newspaper editorializes, "A stout strip vigorously used at home can often do more good than repeated summonses to adolescent courts. It can and should also be used on parents themselves when obviously needed to drive home plain parental duty."

More sensible advice comes from Benjamin Fine, formerly education editor of the *New York Times*, in *1,000,000 Delinquents*. Though Fine is fully aware of the increase in juvenile delinquency, he refuses to surrender to hysteria and adopt the woodshed panacea. Fine writes, "The (woodshed) attitude . . . at its worst and most dangerous, is emotion (in the objectionable sense), reactive rather than thoughtful. It represents the type of identity thinking that we share with the lower animals. Teenage purse snatcher with slipknife-evil-crime-fear-Hate! Hit him over the head! Lock him up! Punish him! Don't care if we kill him! . . . The woodshed technique may be valuable or even necessary in some few instances. But to advocate it, as some do, as a general philosophy, will do considerably more harm than good. . . . There is no evidence that severe punishment of itself given to children or their parents has any effect whatsoever in curbing juvenile delinquency. Conversely it is difficult to measure its ill effects."

Dr. Leonard W. Mayo, chairman of the National Mid-Century Committee, has pointed out that it takes more than just a strapping to cure delinquency. Corporal punishment may merely harden the delinquent in his belief that he is alone in the world and that he has been deserted. Potential and actual juvenile delinquents need understanding more than flogging.

Naturally, the advocates of the return to the woodshed are among the severest critics of modern programs of education. Their editorial spokesmen satirically deride "the bleeding hearts who say education is the answer." A favorite whipping boy is "progressive education." So it is good to hear one of America's great deans of education, Ernest O. Melby, respond: "In a democratic society, the only effective discipline in the long run is self-discipline. It was self-discipline that the progressive school sought to teach and in its best form actually did teach successfully. In some substantial degree practice in self-discipline has found its way into a large proportion of American schools and to the degree that it has been adopted it is a prevention of juvenile delinquency. Unfortunately not nearly as many schools as one might hope for have adopted such disciplinary practices. Therefore, to whatever degree education is responsible for juvenile delinquency, it is the persistence of the 'old school' with its failure to meet the needs of children that is more to blame than the adoption of the newer procedures."

Justine Wise Polier, for two decades a justice in New York City's Domestic Relations Court, has noted an interesting similarity between the drives of the get-tough spokesmen and those who attack modern schools. "It is not surprising that those who would indulge their desire to get tough with children and punish parents are those who scorn the long tedious process of education and are also among the vanguard of those who are attacking our schools today. In these attacks one finds the same drive to secure conformity and docility through force (sometimes euphemistically called discipline); the same drive to control from the outside; and the same lack of faith in the possibilities of education to help children and adults alike learn self control and their responsibilities and rights in a democratic society."

The woodshed panacea is at best debatable even when conceived only as an emergency measure to curb and control a slum area which has temporarily gotten out of hand. But as a national proposal for the prevention and cure of juvenile delinquency, it is tragically misguided. Juvenile delinquency is complex, variously caused and variously prevented. Many of society's agencies must team up to contribute to prevention and control.

The good modern school is one among several agencies which can contribute to prevention and cure of juvenile delinquency. Actually and potentially, it is a far more effective agency than the return to the woodshed. This is no sentimental claim; instead, it is based on what we know of the nature of the delinquent.

Good schools with modern programs are needed for all children. But they are particularly needed for the present or the potential delinquent. According to research well-summarized by Kvaraceus, the life of the delinquent is more likely than that of the nondelinquent to be characterized by:

Living in slum areas
Overcrowded, poorly furnished and badly kept homes
Poverty and deprivation
Bad home conditions
No family recreation

Parents less interested in his future
Home characterized by quarreling, rejection and indifference
Discipline, if not completely lacking, depending heavily on physi-
cal punishment
Less mental ability
Ten points lower than nondelinquents on IQ scales
Instability
Resentment of authority
Emotional conflicts
Inclination to look for adventure away from home
Disliking school
Lacking career plans
Doing poorly in school
Receiving low grades
Failing to be promoted
Behaving badly
Escaping through truancy.

The delinquent reacts to his inner problems with outward aggressive behavior in a society which finds his conduct bothersome
and contrary to how life should be lived.

There are two central questions in regard to the school's contribution to prevention and control of delinquency. "What kind
of school does America need?" "Will America support the kind
of school it needs?" This article will deal primarily with the first
question.

How can a school help the potential or actual delinquent to
live democratically as a worthy citizen?

The modern school can create an atmosphere in which democracy has a chance to thrive. This is an atmosphere of acceptance,
belongingness, affection, being wanted. Delinquents definitely
need such an atmosphere. Delinquents are short on acceptance
and understanding. They do not find it in their homes. Too often
they find it only in the antisocial behavior of their gang. They
will not find it in an inadequate school where coldness, suspicion
and tension are in the very air, and where rigidity and unneces-
sary restrictions rule.

A modern school can build democratic citizenship through
giving children a chance to take part. Youngsters learn team-
work through working in groups with others, through speaking

out frankly in discussions, through taking part in extracurricular activities such as athletics, band, clubs. To help the active and adventurous delinquent, the modern school stressing participation is preferable to the inadequate school where the children sit passively while the teacher tells them exactly what to do, and exactly how to do it.

If America is to have citizens fit for a democracy, rather than personalities like cowed slaves of communism, America needs modern schools which work toward the self-discipline which is characteristic of the democratic man. Obviously, controls are necessary and they exist in a good modern school. But when possible, the student takes part in setting the rules. Good schools have student councils and governments. Steadily the good teacher, like the good parent, expands the limits of freedom, the area of self-discipline. The inadequate school which struggles to keep the lid on through autocratic discipline engages in bitter eternal warfare with the increasingly rebellious delinquent.

A good modern school can contribute to democratic living through a program which develops a wide range of interests. Potential delinquents need outlets for activity, for expression, for adventure. They need to come in contact with a widening world. The inadequate school which attempts to fill all free hours of potentially delinquent youngsters with extra and increased homework rather than attempts to develop self-propelling, enduring interests is on a dead-end road.

If we are to build better school programs to contribute to the fight against delinquency, we need schools with modern programs geared to individuals.

A good modern school has a curriculum which includes vocational education, work experience, remedial instruction such as remedial reading. It includes twentieth-century offerings like general mathematics, industrial subjects, home economics, physical education, and agriculture—subjects which scarcely existed in 1900. Many classes in a modern school help people to come to grips with their personal and social problems. A program of varied offerings gives the delinquent a better chance to get something out of school.

We must not forget that the typical delinquent is a slower

learner than others. He needs remedial help. He also needs vocational education and work experience.

The formal classical curriculum of abstract bodies of knowledge has little meaning for the delinquent. Formal college entrance programs have no relationship to his life. However capable the college scholars a school produces, it is an inadequate school if it requires an inappropriate curriculum for many of its youngsters, including potential or present juvenile delinquents.

A modern school provides for the individual student abundant opportunities for guidance. Guidance comes best through both specialized guidance personnel and through classroom teachers themselves. In a good school, records are kept. Systematic testing supplies background. Case studies are made.

A delinquent needs somebody who will listen. If the guidance personnel also can turn to specialized services when needed, great possibilities for social betterment through the schools open up. To point out that the juvenile delinquent in particular needs guidance and allied help is to emphasize the obvious. An inadequate school, which has no guidance facilities, loses its great opportunity to help the delinquent.

A good school does its best to see that everyone has some success in the things that an individual is able to do, rather than is penalized for failing to succeed in things which by sheer biological make-up the individual is unable to do. The delinquent needs success, not endlessly repeated failure. In an inadequate school, he fails again and again. Low in ability, he is expected to read at the same rate and understanding as the better equipped students. He becomes the conspicuous class "boob." Repeated failure contributes to drop-outs.

All too many of our children drop out before completing high school. The chances of court appearances are about one in four for school drop-outs and only one in fifty for those enrolled. To fight delinquency, we need more good modern schools which have holding power, not inadequate schools which lose many students through dropping out.

The school can also acquaint all the youngsters within its reach with the pressing social realities of their times.

Specifically, schools can develop programs of family education,

helping all boys and girls to understand the problems and potentialities of the American family. Poor family living makes a great
deal of difference in the creation of delinquents. Young people
can study the total problems of recreation so that they, today
as young people and tomorrow as adults, can increasingly improve recreational opportunities for all, including potential delinquents.

Many good modern schools also help young people to look
directly at their problems of personal living. Youths should understand themselves, their relationships with other boys and girls;
understand racial and nationality backgrounds; understand
delinquency itself. This is a type of group guidance which develops greater self-insight. It is a mental health program which
becomes part of the regular content of the classroom.

But these activities will not be engaged in by an inadequate
school which conceives its instruction to have nothing to do with
the actual ongoing life of a young person in society.

In answering the question, "What kind of school does America need if we are to prevent and control juvenile delinquency?"
emphasis has been placed on a good school with a modern curriculum.

Obviously, the school has still other contributions. For instance, the school plant should be used by young and old outside
of school hours. Early identification of potential delinquents and
consequent handling and referral are of high importance. The
development of parent education can be of great help. Above all,
the school's efforts should be part of a total planned all-commu-
nity attack by coordinated agencies.

"Will America support the kind of school it needs?" Who
could close without pointing out the crucial importance of this
question? Two things are urgently needed: public understanding and financial support.

School men can develop the kind of modern school described
here only if the people, to whom the schools belong, understand
its necessity. If the citizenry demands good schools with a modern program of education to meet the challenge of delinquency,
good education will prevail. If, instead, the citizenry permits or

even demands inadequate practices, these will prevail with unfortunate results.

The schools cannot do their jobs without financial support. In America today we are desperately short of teachers. We are even shorter of good teachers who understand children. Our insufficient classrooms are overcrowded. Our classes are too large for individualization. We haven't space for all the children of the American people. We haven't the funds to set up sufficient special services. We haven't the money to make inadequate schools into good modern schools.

꜅ *It is appropriate that* The Intellectually Gifted Child *should appear in the last issue of* Progressive Education *ever to be published, 1956. Throughout its many and often distinguished years of publication,* Progressive Education *was the defender of the gifted against the mediocrity of traditional instruction. I suspect that year after year the gifted child had no firmer journalistic supporter than* Progressive Education *and no more vigorous organizational spokesman than the Progressive Education Association. Always caricatured by its foes and often misinterpreted by its friends (as John Dewey himself pointed out), the progressive movement spoke for the individual and against conformity and docile adjustment long before today's intellectuals found their testament in* The Organization Man *and* The Lonely Crowd.

25 *The Intellectually Gifted Child*

WHAT is a gifted child? A child whose performance is remarkable in any valuable line. So gifted children include not only brilliant youngsters, but also the creative, the inventive, any "remarkable" child. This review deals particularly with three approaches and three issues in the education of the intellectually gifted child.

In American education, conflicting approaches have been suggested for realizing more fully the potentiality of the intellectually gifted. The first approach is termed "enrichment." Staying in the same classes with his less able classmates, the gifted child is given opportunities for developing his skills of investigation, working independently, contributing creatively, participating more fully in planning, having first-hand experiences, engaging in extensive reading, leading groups, contributing maximally to committee work. The teacher's responsibilities include giving the gifted child individual attention, holding him to high standards, and helping him work up to the level of his potential ability.

A second approach to the intellectually gifted child is termed "special grouping." Here the ablest are separated from the less gifted. The separation may range all the way from a special school for gifted children, to a separate program for the gifted within a school, to separate classes for part of a school day, to ability grouping within a class, to an occasional special project designed especially for the gifted.

A third approach to meeting the problem of the intellectually gifted child is termed "acceleration." This may take the form of a child skipping a grade, thus jumping from one heterogeneous group on one grade level to another heterogeneous group further advanced. Acceleration also takes the form of condensing the years of schooling, as, for instance, reducing eight years to seven, reducing the three year junior high school span to two, reducing the normal four years of high school to three. Still another form of acceleration is early admission to college.

Each viewpoint cites successes. Those who call for enrichment cite articles by creative teachers, such as an English teacher who sponsors for gifted children a program of independent reading and creative pursuits and projects in the mass media. They may point to a science teacher who sponsors science clubs, summer jobs, after-school experiences, special coaching, and participation in national talent searches. The protagonists of special grouping cite research studies on grouping experiments. They laud specific classes such as the Los Angeles life science approach through which the twenty-five top students are placed together for a second semester of the required class and then experience an intensive chemistry and physics course. The proponents of acceleration cite the support of the Ford Foundation which has invested in school-college plans and early admission programs for college; they cite the record of younger entrants, who are more likely to graduate from college, who have better academic records, more honors and less disciplinary problems. .

Each of these three approaches (enrichment, special grouping, and acceleration) has opponents as well as proponents. Discussions of these varying viewpoints sometimes degenerate into recriminations. To make an intelligent judgment concerning which approach or combination, if any, is preferable, one must face up to several major issues.

1. Is enrichment an unattainable mirage in today's educational desert of inadequate support for schools?

Some say yes. They argue that enrichment is only a pretty dream in a harsh reality of rising class size, inadequate preparation and high turnover of teachers, lack of books, equipment, and special services. As a result, the intellectually gifted child in the heterogeneous class is in actuality the forgotten child.

Some say no. They admit the obstacles to individualization which exist. But they call for attack on the conditions, rather than acceptance of defeat. They reject false substitutes for skilled and sensitive teachers who individualize instruction in classes in which each person is recognized as different and important.

2. It is undemocratic to separate students in schools on the basis of intelligence quotients?

Some say yes. They argue that separate classes smack of a caste system, that separation breeds snobbishness, that Americans must learn to live and work together with people of varied religions, races, nationalities, and social classes. They argue that recent research has shown that I.Q. stratifications often simply reflect social stratifications. For instance, children from privileged homes have a head start in cultural background, thus raising their scores.

Some argue no to the idea that grouping by intellect is undemocratic. They say that the bane of democracy is equalitarian notions with respect to the intellect. They urge that to educate each to his highest capacity and to recognize realistically the existence of individual differences is the essence of democracy.

3. Is social maladjustment the price of acceleration?

Some say yes. They point to individual cases of maladjusted, bookish prodigies. They argue that it is not a brain but a total personality which is proposed for acceleration and that the risk of social immaturity is high. They add that going from a classroom which is not enriched and which is replete with busy work on a particular grade level to another class on a higher level which also lacks enrichment and is replete with busy work does not actually challenge the gifted young learner.

But some say no to the contention that acceleration has undesirable consequences in the form of social immaturity. They point to Terman's classic study of gifted children in the 1920's and his follow-up in 1947, *The Gifted Child Grows Up*. Terman concluded that his gifted children, many of whom were accelerated, became, in general, highly mature and responsible adults. He concluded that children of 135 I.Q. and over should be promoted to permit college entrance by seventeen at the latest and indicated that a majority would be better off to enter college at sixteen. Incidentally, when Terman's recommendation was checked with representative school men, just about half of the public school administrators favored his proposal while half opposed it.

Based on their conclusions on these three major issues, people take various positions on the proposed approaches.

The advocates of enrichment call for a high degree of individualization in a program of creative modern teaching within heterogeneous classrooms. The opponents say that while this conception is laudable in theory, it is seldom achieved in practice due to overcrowded classrooms and lack of master teachers and equipment.

The advocates of special classes say that children will gain markedly in academic achievement, that they will be stimulated by being associated with fellow-gifted, and that they will not experience any undesirable social discrimination. The opponents regard separate classes as another type of undesirable segregation, perpetuating class distinctions, robbing the average student of the stimulation of those of greater ability.

As to acceleration, its advocates say that the feared social maladjustment simply does not come about, that it is a good thing for people to enter college early and that they do better when this occurs, that early entrance into professional fields gives a longer and more productive lifetime of accomplishment, that young manpower is needed in our society. The opponents of acceleration say that without enrichment acceleration can be uninspiring and that the risk of social immaturity is not worth the expected gain.

Decisions on the major issues should be made in the light of both social philosophy and substantial research. Our magnificient minority of gifted children must not be cheated. Their situation calls for high statesmanship on educational policy and careful consideration of accumulating research. The time has come for an open-minded reassessment of our approaches to intellectually gifted children and, inevitably, the issues sketched above must be faced.

≈§ The social studies were my first love. Since first loves are precious, I can generate considerable steam over the failure of conventional social studies instruction to make history in particular the exciting learning experience for young people that it should be. The fault is a fundamental one, involving basic assumptions on the relative importance of chronology versus solving of problems based on social realities, needs, and democratic values. I hold the latter assumption to be basic. The yearbook editor for the National Council for the Social Studies was tolerant toward my dissenting opinion and gave me space in The Study and Teaching of American History *for my strictures on contemporary history teaching. Condensed from my chapter and occasionally modified by second thoughts, my viewpoint appears below.*

26 *The Teaching of American History*

CAN curricular experiences in American history deal with the real problems of young people, bring into focus the social realities of our time, and steadily illuminate the democratic way? Such are the characteristics of curricular experiences which afford our best opportunities for the development of democratic attitudes.

Applying this test to American history, we find many courses which, when weighed in the balance, are sadly wanting. Despite the emphasis of the "new" history, despite insights from contemporary education, a dreary parade of dates, warriors, and politicians too often continues to masquerade as functional history. In the spirit of "his not to reason why," many students in American history classes today are desultorily memorizing the succession of Presidents and, for examination purposes, regurgitating details of military and political campaigns. There is not a vital curricular experience in a carload of such instruction. It bears no relationship to understanding or practicing democracy. It bears no relation to the pressing social realities of the day. It bears no relation to student needs.

Students are learning through such instruction. But what? They are learning to hate history. They are learning to avoid future thinking about wars or politics or economic affairs. They are learning to go through their paces docilely at the command of a taskmaster. As a recent survey showed, they are learning to forget rapidly. This is their attitudinal training in the Critical Century.

Yet there exist American history courses taught by competent teachers who are more impressed by psycho-logic than the logic of adult-ordered subject matter, who link the past to present social situations, and who use life problems to foster value formation and democratic practice. In such classes the story of the American dream comes alive. The documents of democracy from the Mayflower Compact to the Atlantic Charter are not dusty papers but are the fervent expressions of principles operative in American behavior today. The men and women who gambled on the democratic dream or threw in their lot with its antagonists are not shadowy myths but breathing, hoping, struggling humans.

In such courses there is no gap between current social realities and an account of the past. One grows out of the other. Each is so intimately associated in the student's mind that today's headlines on peace-making blend in with his knowledge of earlier efforts for a lasting peace. Today's story of a ranting racist demagogue creates not confusion but renewed democratic allegiance at the recollection of intolerance in American history.

In such courses the pressing problems of the student's daily life serve as a springboard for learning. History is a well from which may be taken much that is needed for understanding problems important here and now to the learner. Needs are met, whether in the areas of international or intercultural understanding, in consumer or vocational education, in adolescents' personal problems of self-understanding or youth's broader social problems of working and warring.

Why is it that such American history teaching in America's schools is so rare as to seem Utopian in the telling? The faculty

room less frequently hears such success stories and more frequently hears sad little anecdotes like the one about the student
who hogged library books to make his report condemning
monopolies. Instead of successful teaching paving the way for
the development of democratic attitudes, we more usually find
procedures which result in the attitudes described by the New
York State Regents' Inquiry. The investigation in New York
demonstrated that the current school curriculum, including substantial amounts of compulsory history, was not successfully
building democratic attitudes. Nor is it only studies by educators that have the same story to tell. For instance, many of
us were startled by the report from Germany on the number of
American soldiers who believed there was a good deal to be said
for Hitler after all. It is obvious that a critical problem of
developing democratic attitudes exists.

One solution for current nihilistic or negative attitudes is
frequently offered. Teach them still more American history,
since American history has staked out attitude-building as one
of its major claims within the school curriculum. We now teach
American history throughout the grade school; we teach it
again in the junior high; we elaborate and expand upon, as
well as repeat, previous teaching in the eleventh or twelfth grade
of high school. We do not get the results we want, whether in
terms of facts or attitudes. Solution: teach still more of the
same. This so-called solution boils down to teaching still more
of what has not been effective in the past. Such a solution is
the current pathetic fallacy. When the motors of a modern
airplane do not function properly, engineers do not advocate
putting still more of the same motors on the plane in hope that
a few will work. Instead, they strip down the failing engines and
look for the flaws. If the flaws cannot be conquered, they build a
new motor. We had best take a lead from the books of the practical men and look for the flaws in the American history course.
What hypotheses have we as to what to examine?

We might well ask whether there is a defect in respect to
the development of values and the practice of democracy. To help
students formulate values, world views must be continuously
contrasted. Students must examine historical events in the light

of varied principles. They must scrutinize the implications and logical consequences of varied beliefs. History abounds with opportunities for value contrasts which can be fruitful if solidly related to needs and social realities.

If ineffective value education proves to be a current defect, what possible remedial action then? American history teachers might best regard value formation and democratic practice as a central task, if our purpose is to build democratic attitudes. Is not value formation as a proposed focus for history teaching preferable to miscellaneous, peripheral, quaint and curious lore? Is not the school as a microcosm of democratic arrangements preferable to the school run on the model of the authoritarian state?

After an examination of our failing motor, the American history course, some inspectors have charged that although history prides itself in dealing with social realities its students see no intimate relations between the saga of the past and the pressing problems of the present. True, all right-minded historians begin their textbooks with a preface which titillates the reader with the expectation that the scroll of the past to be unrolled in the ensuing pages will enlighten him on the riddles of the present. "The present grows out of the past." And no doubt it does. But if his book contains keys to the cryptograph of the present all too often they are too well hidden and the historian's secrets are safe, at least from high school students.

The remedy may lie in being more outspoken and less wary. Let historians and, more especially, teachers of history labor harder to be more explicit on the relations of past and present. Focusing on the past, ignoring the present, and praying for carry-over is dubious strategy. Let us relate the present complexities in building a workable peace to historical investigation of world courts and leagues of nations. Let us in our teaching draw parallels. Let us teach the Monroe Doctrine and our relationship with South America in such a way that each recurring Latin American crisis would not appear novel and soluble only on the basis of expediency.

Some declare the failing in the American history motor to be a failure to communicate. The flaw, they say, is the failure of a subject matter course, proceeding chronologically, to relate itself to the needs, problems, tensions, and concerns of the student. Value formation and social realities, if taught, are taught as abstractions and fail to come to life because they have little relation to the lives of the learner. In front of the classroom teacher are young people who have problems and needs which are the basic realities of their lives. By the very fact of their being adolescents they have deeply rooted drives. By the fact of their being adolescents in the contemporary American culture, they have culturally-created problems such as concern over jobs, reactions to war, interest in buying.

Instead of capitalizing upon the problems of adolescents, which are broadly social as well as intimately personal in scope, American history teaching too often ignores them. Sensing a need for motivation, teachers substitute drama, sometimes vaudeville, in an attempt to make history absorbing. But showmanship, divorced from real concern, cannot turn the trick. Much of our ingenuity now goes into devices. It might be better used in approaches based on understanding of the problems of adolescents in American culture.

Perhaps American history courses can be modified to deal with the real problems of young people, to bring into focus the social realities of our time, and to steadily illuminate the democratic way. Perhaps American history courses can meet the three educational necessities for successful attitude-building. If the flaws in the motor cannot be remedied, American education may come to depend on other models. If the American history course cannot be used to develop democratic attitudes, it may find itself in the position James Truslow Adams attributed to the dinosaur. The dinosaur, it will be recalled, became extinct through its failure in efficiency and adjustment. If American education continues the practice of retaining subject matter dinosaurs while breath exists in their bodies, non-functional history may become vestigial, sharing with subjects like Latin an elective position in the curriculum. Perhaps now is the time for American history teachers to take some long, slow, and careful looks into their motors. To fly in this age all engines had best be functioning.

⚗ The insights of group dynamics are essentially simple. It is rather too bad that some of the scholars have seen fit to wrap good ideas in a peculiar pedaguese which results in mumbled communication. Stripped of the jargon, here are some approaches to improving human relations in the school program. Though addressed directly to teachers, the insights also should be helpful in many group meetings in which people must work well with each other.

27 *Improving Human Relations in the School Program*

"PRACTICE what you preach!"

"What you do speaks so loudly I can hardly hear what you say."

These old folk sayings are still helpful for modern man. Horse sense is still needed even in a jet age. Even? Especially.

The grand old man of American education, William Heard Kilpatrick, once said, "They learn what they live." His sentence, packed with insight, has already been added to the accumulated wisdom of our people.

Such adages apply strikingly to the improvement of human relations in the school program. For, if you and I are to improve our working relationships, we must learn what we live, practice what we preach, and know that what we do speaks so loudly that people cannot hear what we say.

So, today in our classrooms, most of us are trying to apply what folk-say has long recognized and research has recently been confirming. Steadily the importance of human relations is being recognized in our work with others besides children—

with other teachers, with the parents of our children, and with the supervisors and administrators who affect our daily work.

For an instance, take meetings of teachers with supervisors and administrators to work on the curriculum. We are learning that the human-relations aspects are of high importance to their success. Sometimes arrangements are bungled by the insensitive and the result may be death to the enterprise. I am still haunted by the memory of one such meeting.

A school system had asked me to serve as a curriculum consultant for a series of meetings intended to result in program improvement. Yet there were three strikes against me before the first meeting had hardly begun. Strike One came when the superintendent called the first meeting at the unholy hour of four on Friday afternoon. So the teachers came to the meeting at the tail end of a long week; they were weary, unrefreshed, and totally "on their own time." Had the meeting been at two in an afternoon earlier in the week, the school officials would have shown that they thought curriculum work was important. The contribution of an hour of school time would have been readily matched by an hour contributed by the teachers.

I knew that Strike Two had whizzed across the plate when I saw the room in which the meeting was to be held. It was an unattractive classroom; the teachers squeezed uncomfortably into small chairs behind screwed-down desks. In the same school, I later found, there was a comfortable library and a home economics suite with chairs which acknowledged adulthood, to say nothing of middle-age spread! In the bare room, there was no serving of coffee and doughnuts or any other inexpensive yet all-important human touch.

The chairman addressed the meeting. "As you all know, all of us here have long been at work developing the curriculum." The expression on the faces of the teachers told me this was news to them. "Now we have with us an expert from the university who will tell us what is wrong with our curriculum and how to change it. I present Dr. Van Til." No one planning the meeting had learned that curriculum change begins with the problems met by the teacher, that change comes through shared experiences, that a consultant is a helper and not an oracle.

Strike Three, and I was out before I had begun. Nothing that I did or said could save the day.

After the meeting, my wife, who had accompanied me to shop in the community, met me in the school doorway. Perspiring profusely, I inquired, "Dear, did you hear anything as the teachers passed you that might help me in my future work here?" Smiling a wifely smile, she responded, "There was that one lady who said as she sailed by, 'So help me Hannah, I'll resign first!'"

I learned a great deal that afternoon about the importance of human relations in the school program!

Sometimes, even with the best intentions, we fail. Take Jane Smith, for instance. She knows that her upper elementary grade students should improve their human relationships. So she has them learn several of the magnificent statements of the American tradition: the opening of the Declaration of Independence, the preamble to the Constitution of the United States, the Gettysburg Address.

But Jane Smith's classroom is a dictatorship in microcosm. From her seat of authority behind her desk, Jane Smith hears recitations from row after row and passes judgment on each response in her little gray book. Only the magnificent phrases break the silence of a classroom atmosphere of tension and obsessive competition in which fear and hostility are born.

So the children learn. But what do they learn? They learn what they live. They learn what they practice rather than what Jane Smith preaches. What Jane Smith does, speaks so loudly that they can scarcely hear what their instructor is saying. Jane Smith has taught the words of democracy. However, the children have learned the music of authoritarianism.

But another teacher, Mary Brown, knows that the song of democratic human relations requires both words and music. In her classroom, she creates an atmosphere in which children feel that they belong, are wanted and accepted, that they too count. The children participate in discussions, committees, decision making, and classroom management. They are respected as persons and so they learn to respect others. They take part in associated living and so they learn to live well with others. As they read and write and talk, they find that ideas can be live and exciting, rather than canned and dull.

Mary Brown's children learn too. They learn what they live. They both intellectualize and live the democratic way of life. What Mary's children do speaks so loudly that it will be built into the very structure of their lives. Nor are the words of democracy neglected. The music and the words are inseparable.

But it is not sentimentality which persuades us that Mary Brown has a better chance than Jane Smith of building better human relationships among her students. Mary Brown's way meets the pragmatic test which Americans customarily use. It works.

Supporting the effectiveness of a democratic atmosphere in improving human relations are the findings of scientific inquiry. And re-enforcing Mary Brown's approach are studies in human development and social engineering. When Detroit schools conducted their Citizenship Education Study, the importance of a democratic atmosphere in the school in developing good citizenship was reaffirmed. When researchers in intercultural and intergroup relations reported their findings in such classics as *The Authoritarian Personality*, the importance of living democratically in classroom and home was stressed. When educators appeared before the Kefauver Committee, they testified again to the role of the school in combating juvenile delinquency through creating a humane environment. The weight of evidence is impressive.

A warm personality helps in the development of effective human relations. But techniques are useful too. The young science of group dynamics offers technical help to anyone who works with groups. For a gathering of mature individuals does not automatically insure the group's functioning in a mature manner.

So we are learning more about the varied roles different personalities play in groups. The best size for a group for a particular purpose is being studied. The existence of hidden agenda is now recognized, the unmentioned problem sometimes on the minds of group members which must be gotten out of the way if effective work on the scheduled agenda is to take place. Group leaders are increasingly being conceived as evokers, stimulators, synthesizers, rather than Machiavellian autocrats or efficiency experts.

We are learning ways of creating a permissive atmosphere in which all are encouraged to take part. Experimentation goes on with sociodrama and role-playing in which individuals are assigned, or volunteer, for parts in a spontaneous acting out of a problem under consideration. Large audiences are being involved in participation through introducing small buzz groups in which everyone has a chance to discuss or develop questions. New ways of feed-back are being developed, by which group conclusions are summarized and group members are kept aware of how the group is doing.

Yet the ground rules for improving human relations in the school program are simpler than the group-dynamics enthusiasts with their colorful jargon would have us believe. They were stated best by two laymen, neither of whom may have ever heard of group processes. They are Carl Sandburg and Jimmy Durante. Sandburg says in *The People, Yes*, "Everybody knows more than anybody." Sandburg is right. Shared thought is necessary for improved human relations. Jimmy Durante says on radio and television, "Everybody wants to get into the act." Jimmy is right too. Under all the shyness and hesitancy, people want to belong, to be involved. The ground rules apply not only to classroom situations, but they apply equally well to teachers working with supervisory staff.

There is really nothing mysterious about improving human relations in or out of the school program. Among the most effective human-relations men I know are an assistant dean of a college and a vice-president of a large magazine publishing company. Both are essentially friendly individuals who enjoy people. Each has the skill and imagination to put himself in the other person's place intellectually, emotionally, almost physically, and to act on what he perceives. They know that people are important.

The road to better human relations winds through a land of

participation and sharing. The characteristic climate is a democratic atmosphere, friendly and humane. Along the way, the travelers practice what they preach, learn what they live. No short cuts have yet been found.

❧ In March 1960, I talked to an assembly of the Association for Supervision and Curriculum Development conference at Washington, D.C. Since the 7000 members had just done me the honor of electing me president-elect, I worked hard to make my talk a comprehensive statement of my views on recent developments and their meaning for the curriculum. I thought the most important aspect of the talk was the case for education for social understanding. The journalists, however, concentrated on my comments on James B. Conant's reports on secondary education. I'll let you judge for yourself.

28 *Social and Cultural Developments Influence the Curriculum*

WHY SHOULD educators be concerned for new social and cultural developments as the nineteen sixties open? Many have put the answer in sober and scholarly fashion but no one has yet said it with more wit and insight than Harold Benjamin in *The Saber-Tooth Curriculum.* You will recall from Benjamin's hilarious fable that New-Fist, the founder of caveman education, devised an eminently sensible curriculum for the children of the cave realm. The three fundamentals—fish grabbing with the bare hands, woolly horse clubbing, and saber-tooth tiger scaring with fire—were in accordance with the demands of the social order and the needs of individuals. But a glacier came down from the north and conditions of life in the cave realm changed drastically. It was no longer possible to grab fish with the bare hands in the now muddy streams; the little woolly horses went far away to the dry highlands; the saber-tooth tigers caught pneumonia and almost became extinct. The wily and agile fish hid under rocks; elusive antelopes replaced the stupid little woolly horses; great bears, unafraid of fire, menaced the tribe in place of the defunct tigers. Without food, hides, and security from sudden death, the tribe nearly perished.

But men of the New-Fist stamp invented a new technology to catch fish with seines, antelopes with snares, bears with pits. Yet the wise old men who controlled the schools insisted on continuing the teaching of fish-grabbing, horse-clubbing, and tiger-scaring—the standard cultural subjects—and rejected as mere training all proposals to teach the cave children the new ways of living.

Sometimes forgotten, even by those of us who cut our educational eye teeth on Benjamin's classic fable, is the inadequacy of the responses of the progressives as well as the inadequacy of the responses of the traditionalists to the new social demands on the cave realm. While the traditionalists insisted that the essence of true education was timelessness, the progressives simply transferred fish-grabbing with the bare hands from the heated school pool to the banks of the real creek. Despite the creative fish-grabbing which developed, it was still no longer possible to grab agile, intelligent fish in muddy waters with the bare hands. Despite creative tiger-scaring through waving brands before two caged, ancient, toothless tigers, the last of their breed, the giant bears which were unafraid of fire still prowled the trails. Progressive school programs in the cave realm refused to recognize the existence and the threat of the giant bears.

Whatever our philosophies, whatever our methodologies, we in education ignore new social and cultural developments at great peril to our group and to the persons who comprise it. This is the still valid message of *The Saber-Tooth Curriculum*.

Today the glacier comes at the Americans not from the north but in the shape of a Soviet colossus from the East probing into space, an ever increasing tide of hungry human beings in underdeveloped nations like India, the soaring growth curves of the Chinese Communists, the chant of FREE-dom from the mouths of African natives. The reason why international problems are paramount in today's social order is clear. International problems present stark matters of life and death for our world, our American society, and for all of the individuals who populate the planet Earth.

A dominating social reality of our times is the continuing conflict between the Western coalition led by the United States and the Communist coalition still led by Russia, though China is beginning to close the gap. This struggle, even when contained within its "peaceful" stage of cold war, readiness economy, diplomatic maneuvering, and bombers either aloft or alert, affects all of us. To Americans, the personal impact comes through military service of young family members; high taxation; an economy oriented toward the big customer, the national government; inflation; economic and military aid abroad; the struggle for the minds of men in a continuing war of nerves; the fateful policy decisions on testing nuclear weapons, on fall-out and radiation, on space probes.

The target of the conflict is increasingly control of outer space as nations strive for domination through extension of the arching span of missiles, through manned space platforms as launching pads.

Always existent is the threat of our uneasy peace deteriorating into total war. Involvement of people would then be global, whether the missiles came from space satellites or earthly land masses. In *On The Beach*, Neville Shute has graphically portrayed the devastation to the point of total extinction which might come to even faraway lands through fall-out and radiation in the event of use of nuclear bombs.

Should lethal bomb explosions be averted, the world will still have to cope with the population explosion and the freedom explosion of the underdeveloped nations. The Population Reference Bureau of Washington, D.C., has pointed that today a nation as large as Italy is added to the world each year. Today there are three billion people on earth; by the year 2000, only 40 years away, a seven billion population is predicted. People in the hungriest lands reproduce most rapidly; in much of tropical Latin America and in parts of Asia, the population will increase 25 times in the twentieth century, given continuance of the present trend.

The people of the underdeveloped nations are caught up in a

freedom explosion that sweeps across the changing map of Africa and Southeast Asia, that simmers under the surface in Latin America and breaks through on Caribbean Islands. Between the Soviet systems of Russia and China and the Western system of North America and Western Europe lie the uncommitted people of the underdeveloped nations. In their third world they live by the millions in Southeast Asia, Oceania, the sub-continent of India, the erupting Middle East and North Africa of Moslem allegiances, an awakening Black Africa, even in a Latin America only insecurely linked with the power to the North. Their decisions, their emerging power systems, may be crucial to the fate of mankind. Though uncommitted to either major power bloc, the people of the underdeveloped nations have their emergent commitments: to new nationalisms, unity of like peoples, industrial growth, rising living standards; and against hunger, imperialism, colonialism, color prejudice, decrepid feudal remnants, control by outsiders. Whose revolution they will adopt, the American or the Russian, whose economy, the mixed or the Communist, whose pattern, the democratic or the authoritarian, is on the lap of the gods. The likely answer is that they will adopt their own versions of revolution, economy, and pattern.

Meanwhile at home in the United States, never has the nation been so rich and so nervous, so wealthy and so socially starved. In the affluent society, paradoxes abound. Americans have achieved a highly developed private production system which provides our expanding middle classes with insolent chariots, chrome-laden, high tail-finned, and too long for metropolitan parking; with T.V. sets equipped with switches controlled from armchairs to eliminate the ubiquitous advertising blare which makes T.V. economically feasible; with surpluses of food which produce obesity which shortens lives which worries insurance companies. Yet Americans starve their social services. In Megalopolis schools are overcrowded; smog stifles breathing; parks are unsafe for walking; streets are littered; parking is prohibited; commuters creep into the City, through the streets, and out of the City. In Suburbia, aromas from over-flowing septic tanks in sewerless communities blend with the grassy smells; the schools are on double sessions; the hospitals are overcrowded. Firemen gallantly respond to an alarm and halt precipitately at the border of one of the 16,000 administrative units of the 174 urban regions to watch a house outside their jurisdiction burn down. Compared to the private production sector, those who man the public sector are underpaid; the more able and alert, unless exceptionally dedicated, switch over to private production. The social balance between public and private enterprises is askew. We have a magnificent supply of some things and a calamitous lack of other things. A punster from Mars might conclude that we are literally the land of the dirty rich.

Pockets of poverty persist in the affluent society. They are yet unreached by big labor or the rising tide of private production. Included in the pockets of the underprivileged are share-croppers, migratory workers, Negroes experiencing job discrimination, Puerto Ricans on the Island and in the mainland mega-lopolises, old people living longer yet encountering earlier a turn away phrase "too old," disabled and handicapped people. Franklin D. Roosevelt's classic 1933 group "ill-fed, ill-housed, ill-clad," has shrunk to one fifth of the nation in 1960. Ironically the section of the nation embracing the highest percentage of the contemporary underprivileged, the South, is the section of the nation most stubbornly resistant to campaigns for the deprived people. Proven again is the Biblical injunction that man does not live by bread alone. Perhaps he also lives by ancient and irrational passions.

On the social-domestic scene of the 1960's, economic growth of the great technology of America is taken for granted. But in the esoteric circles of the economically literate, the debate focuses on the rate of growth. Historically, our rate of production growth has been three per cent; in general, our current growth rate as the 50's yield to the 60's is two and one-half per cent, we are told. Yet as the curves of Chinese production rise sharply so that the total volume of China's industrial output—especially heavy industrial output—is far ahead of the Soviet Union's at the beginning of the 1930's, as Khrushchev insists that the Russians will bury us—at least economically—doubt grows that the American growth rate is sufficient. Peiping asserts that in 1959 its total industrial and agricultural output grew by thirty-one per cent over 1958. Moscow claims the Soviet Union's national income rose eight per cent in 1959. Granted possible unreliability of Chinese and Russian sources and granted that these nations have a great distance to go to match American productivity, uneasiness still persists as to the adequacy of the present two and one-half per cent growth in the United States. Economists of politically liberal persuasion in the United States call for a four and one-half per cent production growth accompanied by a renaissance of the starved social services. Economists of conservative political bent characterize the combination as Utopian. Some urge that we must choose between production growth and expanded social services. The liberals respond that a nation which created the World War II production miracle by rejecting Hermann Goering's choice of guns or butter through producing both in heroic quantities, need not make such a Hobson's choice.

In a few short centuries science and its mechanical accompaniments have changed the developed nations of the world from agricultural, aristocratic, scarcity systems to industrial, welfare, high production systems. The underdeveloped nations will follow the same course as rapidly as they can manage it if they can get a start and manage to control their population. The influence of the age of science on the United States has been especially notable; a land that was wilderness a few centuries ago has become a technological complex with automation on the horizon. Historically, America has stressed technology, application, know-how, rather than abstraction, theory, broad principles. Americans borrowed ideas from Europeans and put them to work. They did not reject with aristocratic contempt the manual aspects of scientific creation, accompanied by dirty hands, sweat, and soiled work clothes. The resultant great technology was characterized by transforming power by way of steam, then electricity, and now nuclear energy for peaceful purposes. In the process, precise machine tools have been developed. Interchangeable parts have been standardized. The belt line system of assembly is now being extended toward automation in which a continuous flow of production is scarcely touched by human hands during the process.

Machines increasingly control the feeding of machines. Robots which act for man come close to the process of thought as they use information for productive purposes.[1]

More than any other man, Henry Ford, with his dedication to machine tools, interchangeable parts, and the assembly line, doomed the pastoral, rural America of the 19th century which he nostalgically reproduced in Greenfield Village. Automation, the logical extension of the Ford belt line idea, is destined to change American life even more drastically. The implications include the rising need for skilled and semi-skilled technicians, accompanying decline to the vanishing point of manual and unskilled labor, the extension of leisure creating a vacuum in man's life to be filled with spectatoritis and alcohol or by participation and cultural development.

In a nation made up of varied ancestral families, of multiple faiths, of a kaleidoscope of skin colors, tensions among groups can exist. This is the case in the United States where practices leading to better human relations conflict with practices characterized by prejudice, discrimination, and group antagonism.

On the side of good human relations are found four of the major forces of our times: the democratic idea of liberty and equality, the Western Judaic-Christian tradition of religion, the findings of scientific inquiry, and the supreme law of the land of the United States.

Yet counter to the great world ideas supporting good human relations exist what might be termed the great passions. The great passions derive from history, for instance from the Civil War-Reconstruction catastrophe rather than the tradition of the Bill of Rights, from the religious wars and the anti-Semitism that racked medieval Europe rather than from the social gospel of the twentieth century, from Know-Nothing movements and restrictive discriminatory immigration laws rather than frontier egalitarianism which accepted a man on merit. The great passions spring from calculation of short-term economic advantage, ranging in scope from the plantation system or an exclusive unionism to a housewife grumbling about a domestic's wages, or a real estate man placing an ad discriminating against members of a particular faith. The great passions also spring from human psychology, from the wellsprings of human personality not yet completely understood.

Discrimination, when it exists, can apply to nearly one-third of the nation; more than 15 million Negroes, 2 million Mexican-Americans, 5 million Jews, 10 million foreign-born whites, 20 million of foreign or mixed parental background are included among the potential targets of discrimination.

The balance sheet as applied to American Negroes, the evident minority, shows a formidable burden of debits throughout history and a growing body of credits in contemporary times. Striking the balance, the American Negro, compared to his white fellow citizen, is poorer, has less education, goes to poorer schools, is barred by color from more cultural opportunities, is booked for more crimes, experiences more illnesses, has less capable medical care, and has a shorter life expectancy. This is a formidable indictment of society. On the positive side, gains have been made through desegregated armed forces; Fair Employment Practices laws in some states; Supreme Court decisions on housing, transportation and education; the intercultural education movement in American schools; a persisting national prosperity in which the Negro shares; growing political power particularly in balance of power situations in Northern and some Southern metropolitan situations; a long series of "firsts" breaking barriers in sports, government, recreation, entertainment, science and other fields.

Discrimination against the foreign-born steadily ebbs, partially through the mixed blessings of restricted immigration and partly as the descendants of the foreign-born move into the main stream of American life. For the most recently arrived, discrimination is real, as many Puerto Ricans are finding today in New York City. But as the descendants of immigrants climb the American success ladder, break through barriers into business, the professions, and the suburbs, assimilation takes place. Indeed, one of the American problems today is avoiding the more insecure and authoritation-oriented among the assimilated from supporting discrimination against the newest arrivals to the American kaleidoscope!

Discrimination against Jews is less open than against Negroes and newcomers. Today anti-Semitic discrimination still takes the form of attempting to bar Jews from social situations, such as certain suburbs, clubs, resorts, or through establishing quotas as in colleges, or through unseen obstacles to employment in some fields and to advancement in others. There continues to exist a vigorous lunatic fringe of anti-Semites who attribute all evils to a Jewish conspiracy. These join with the color racists in situations of violence and pressure both in Southern school-related situations and Northern metropolitan agitation.

In today's social order two of the most complex intergroup problems are desegregation of schools and living with religious differences. The desegregation of schools problem is particularly vexing in two locales which are not commonly coupled because they represent different geographical orders: the South and Suburbia. The problem of living with religious differences arises because, despite substantial similarities, religious differences do exist and will persist and even quite possibly sharpen in a four faith society: Protestant, Catholic, Jewish, and unaffiliated.

Though the decision of the Supreme Court that segregation of public schools is contrary to the law of the land was reached in 1954, there was by early 1960 no desegregation of schools in Louisiana, Alabama, Mississippi, Georgia, and South Carolina. Only token desegregation had taken place in Florida, North Carolina, Virginia, Tennessee, and Arkansas. The question inevitably arises both at home and abroad whether Americans intend to live by their democratic principles. Less dramatic and thus far less likely to make the headlines is the stubborn resistance of Suburbia, definitely including Northern suburbs, to "outsiders", a comprehensive term which often includes anyone who cannot qualify as white, middle class, and nominally Christian. As a result, suburban schools often attempt to teach social sensitivity, better human relations, and democracy in a one race, one class, one religious tradition setting—a quixotic enterprise. Yet the pressures are remorseless as the "undesirable elements," as many suburbanites might class them, break out of their slums and ghettos. The ramparts are already gone; the invaders have spilled into the inner suburbs; the tide is lapping at the outer suburbs as the truly exclusive flee to the exurbs. Where after the exurbs? Perhaps outer space.

Such are a sampling of new developments in the social order. The American attitudes which arise in response to these times might be classified in various ways. One useful dimension is to divide Americans as to attitudes into the complacent and the worried.

Many hard-bitten observers believe that the complacent have inherited the American earth. As a politician put it in Maxwell Anderson's play, *Both Your Houses,* "the resources of the American people for apathy have scarcely been tapped."

The complacent, when roused to articulation, point out that economically never did the American people have it so good. The mills and the factories roar and the crops of the fertile fields overflow the bins for storage of excess farm products. All the prophets agree that the indices point upward. Jobs are abundant; the employer shakes hands with the job applicant, surreptitiously feels his pulse, and employs him if it is beating, however faintly. The coffee break of the secretary grows longer and threatens to swallow what used to be termed the working day. The multiple manhattans and martinis enrich the executive's lengthening lunch hours.

Peace is wonderful too. The only wars are little wars. Even these are sometimes reminiscent of operettas; in Algeria, for instance, the French generals frantically switched sides while the Moslem sheiks waited in the wings for their cues. The statesmen tour the world assuring all in earshot of their undying affection for the dove of peace. The Hungarian refugees, whose crude banners scream "murderers" at the distinguished visiting Russians, seem oddly archaic and certainly bad-mannered in the new era. Korea seems a long time ago. Today father knows best.

The worried, however, dissent. On the international scene they point to the space lag and the missile gap. Their grim joke has it that when we get to the moon we will have to go through the Russian customs. They are troubled by the power of the Chinese example as perceived by the underdeveloped nations. India is the potential counterargument but that nation is plagued by population pressures, persisting poverty, and border vulnerability. Bearing his foreign aid and industrial products, the American, an innocent abroad, may be received as a Greek bearing gifts. Burdick and Lederer suggest two possible images in their widely read *The Ugly American*. One is the technician who was physically ugly, yet practical, adaptable, multi-lingual and beloved. The other was the book's truly Ugly American, the politician who clung to his golden ghetto, aloof, provincial, the target of everyone's wit, illiterate of the language, ignorant of the ways of the foreign lands which were his Siberias for temporary comfortable exile.

The worried see the American scene as less than a Utopia. They point to the starved social services in a land where private enterprise frantically innovates such novelties as golden toothpicks for the man or woman who has everything. As they study America's growth rate, they hear echoes of Lloyd George's poignant phrase, "too little and too late."

The impasses in the South and in Suburbia trouble many. Some wonder whether the favorable impact on world opinion through the Supreme Court decision of 1954 is dissipated by America's looking the other way throughout the later 1950's. Others, concerned for the American soul rather than the international image alone, ask whether we are not attempting to serve two masters simultaneously by developing a home-grown hypocritical lip-worship of human dignity and equality which is accompanied by a comfortable practice of segregation and discrimination in our personal lives. What they regard as a nibbling away at separation of church and states worries still other observers.

But perhaps the basic underlying concern of today's worried is the prevalence of complacency. The reformers of the 1930's were concerned primarily about predatory exploitation, callousness to welfare values, the unchecked power of a variety of robber barons. To a mid-century generation of intellectuals, however, the threat to democracy seems to be a grey anonymity, a nation of other-directed personalities, of organization men, of conformist status seekers, of dependents on tranquilizers, of manipulators of group process, of prophets of uncritical adjustment to the status quo, of passive security-minded denizens of a Brave New World, an Animal Farm, a 1984.

In the last half of the twentieth century the peril to the dynamic democratic experiment, to the permanent American Revolution, seems to the worried intellectual only superficially external. He suspects that it is both internal and external. For he knows that it is part of the Communist theory to rely on internal weaknesses in the practice of the democratic idea. The Communists hope that the internal failure of the democratic experiment in America and in the world will do their work for them. As their guarantee that the world will fall like ripe fruit into their hands, the Marxists, true to their prophet, rely upon the collapse of capitalism, recurring economic depression, fondness for imperialist exploitation, in contrast to high Soviet production, rising living standards of backward peoples in the Soviet orbit, know-how in cultivating international relationships. The Communists regard as essentially hypocritical American values of respect for the worth and dignity of the individual, of liberty and freedom, of egalitarianism, and of fraternity. In refutation they cite undemocratic practices by Americans, segregation of the American Negro, the plight of slum dwellers, persisting maldistribution of wealth, vestiges of industrial feudalism, starved social services (especially education) in an affluent society, callousness toward underdeveloped nations, use of foreign aid as an instrument of military policy, superior attitudes of Americans abroad. The Communists regard our undemocratic practices as certain to doom our democratic protestations.

The overwhelmingly obvious implication of new social and cultural developments is the crucial need for education for social understanding. Upon the solution of our international problems —the conflict between the Western and the Communist worlds, the space explosion, the population explosion, the freedom explosion—depends the physical existence of mankind. The issue is starkly and literally life or death. Upon the solution of our domestic-economic problems—an affluent society with poverty pockets and starved social services, an inadequate growth rate, an oncoming automation—depends the quality of existence of Americans. The issue is no less than the kind of civilization we create in America. Upon the solution of our intercultural problems—the great passions which sabotage the great world ideas, the speed of change in the balance sheet for minorities, the sharpening of religious differences—depends the moral existence of Americans in the eyes of the world and ourselves. The issue is whether or not we intend to live by our democratic creed and heritage.

To achieve the degree of social understanding imperative, we need mobilization of the potentialities of the total general education curriculum as we have never needed it before. So formidable a task cannot be delegated to the social studies alone. The social insight required calls for knowing both world people and the American kaleidoscope through reading, including literature, and for expressing aspiring and humane values worthy of a great civilization through communication skills, including writing. Developing the ability to share ideas with people of other lands through talking another world language and understanding other cultures becomes desirable. Social understanding calls for appreciating the creative expressions of people of other cultures and actively contributing to creativity, thus joining in the great fraternity of art. Physical education and recreation are needed to develop enduring leisure pursuits in an age of automation and to develop the international and intercultural fellowship that can stem from games and sports. The social understanding necessary calls for the comprehension of the achievements and threats in the realms of science and mathematics; for sharing the awareness which has caused our more perceptive scientists to recognize human implications in their endeavors as the atomic clock ticks on toward midnight. And clearly the crucial need for social understanding calls for a problem-oriented social studies program which uses the social sciences as resources rather than allows itself to be enslaved by chronologies. Today's urgent problems require a socially oriented program of general education which coordinates insights from many fields, integrating many disciplines in the interest of urgent social understanding.

In addition to the crucial need for social understanding which should be met through general education, a varied program of special education is made necessary by the new social and cultural developments. Special education is particularly needed to meet new vocational demands.

In an age of science, children and youth must learn the

language of science and mathematics as part of today's literacy demanded by the times. But in addition to such general education in science and mathematics, an increasing proportion of our youth will become technicians—a general term used here for those who need more than general education in science and mathematics because of vocational necessities. Today, in a world sadly deficient in social understanding, the call for technicians is for war-related programs. But even if the Soviet Union and its allies were to vanish miraculously from the face of the earth, more technicians would still be needed in our technological society moving toward automation. Manual labor is decreasing; the production worker who ranges in training from semi-skilled to key scientist is increasingly in demand.

Just as the great technology demands more technicians, it demands still other vocational abilities. Since fewer people will be needed for the manual aspects of production, more and more will be needed in recreation, education, health, welfare and a host of service-related occupations. With redirection of part of the energies and wealth of an affluent society, a tremendous development in the presently starved social services will follow. In a society which works fewer hours and increases leisure time, a renaissance of the many arts seems in the making. The social understanding which we must increasingly achieve if, literally, we are to survive will result in the flowering of occupations which are comparatively dormant today, such as planning for the new relationships of Megalopolis and Suburbia, educating the underdeveloped people of the world, maintaining the peace through international agencies.

In short, new social and cultural developments are leading to a variety of vocations for Americans. Some young Americans now in school will become technicians, relying heavily on specialized science and mathematics backgrounds. Some will become workers in the social services, the arts, the new fields created by the need for social understanding. Some will follow long-established vocations, since law, business, transport, commercial recreation, and myriad other established vocations are not likely to go the way of the blacksmith, despite social change.

Consequently, a balanced curriculum which stresses individual differences is the logical outgrowth of the new social and cultural developments. Balance among the content areas is needed if we are to have a fighting chance of achieving the social understanding to which all areas contribute. Recognition of individual differences as part of balanced opportunities for specialism is needed if we are to help young people move into the emerging occupational patterns which require technicians, arts and social service personnel, and long-established vocations which will persist.

Balance as to the foundations of a good curriculum is needed too. For if the new social and cultural developments counsel us to take into account the social realities of our times in curriculum building, nothing in the new developments minimizes the psychological and philosophical foundations of the curriculum. Indeed, in an era in which social understanding is imperative, the importance of a psychologically-sensitive education which meets the individual needs of children and youth and relies on valid insights into how persons learn is enhanced, not diminished. The importance of a philosophically-oriented education which stresses the practice and intellectualization of democratic values, including respect for individual personality, working together for common purposes, and the rigorous use of the method of intelligence, is increased. Concern for social realities without the psychological insights which enable us to communicate with the learner and without the values which provide a sense of direction will not result in greater social understanding.

Ironically, the new social and cultural developments have not led to a public or professional crusade for social understanding through general education nor to advocacy of preparation for varied vocations through special education. Instead a spectacular aspect of the new social and cultural developments initiated the Great Panic of 1957. For in the fall of 1957 the Russians sent Sputniks soaring into space. In America, the panic button was pushed. As satellites orbited in space, extreme ideas were voiced in our land. Our nation was described as though it were technologically illiterate; this nation which in three centuries had converted a wilderness into the most advanced industrial society the world had ever known, this nation which had pioneered on the land, under the sea, and in the air. American education was portrayed as a colossal failure. To extremists, the Soviet Union became the exemplary educational model. Apparently anything the Russians did in education was right; everything we had done in American education was wrong.

Crash programs for the immediate mass production of scientists and mathematicians were demanded. Conceptions of an elite, often with accompanying overtones of aristocratic society, were advanced. The class-perpetuating European system of education, with examination-dictated divisions during childhood into leaders and led, was seriously proposed.

The unscholarly scholars quickly latched on to Sputnik's tail. The unscholarly scholars, a small but noisy minority among the genuine scholars taking part in the current Great Debate on education, seem to think that in some mysterious way they personally are exempted from the demands of scholarship by the mere act of departure from their own disciplines.

The unscholarly scholars, some in high places, reached for the headlines and the air waves with irresponsible assertions that comically-titled courses have taken over the high school curriculum. Currently, their favorite comedy gems seem to be tap dancing, baby sitting, co-ed cooking, fly casting, and something called personality courses. Perhaps it is more than a coincidence that the unscholarly scholars seldom name schools. From now on when the unscholarly comics talk about the strange courses that have taken over the high school curriculum, educators had better ask "where?" and press for book, chapter and verse. If there are any responses, scrutinize them closely.

We learned the importance of this from Alhambra High School, California. A column in *The New York Herald-Tribune*, February 11, 1958, reported that a Los Angeles County high school had received upon demand equal national television time from a major broadcasting system.

"Alhambra High School took exception to the picture drawn of the school on the ninety-minute telecast, "Where We Stand," on January 5. On the network show, which contrasted the Soviet and American struggle for supremacy, four Alhambra High boys were interviewed on film, and three of them said they were taking 'co-ed cooking' courses . . .

"The program's narrator . . . then called Alhambra 'typical of most of our schools' and said that 'in secondary and grammar schools our courses tend to be soft.'

"On Sunday's show . . . Mr. Strother, the principal, will point out that only thirty-three of the 1,030 boys at Alhambra take the one-semester elective course in co-ed cooking. Mr. Strother will also say that half of the school's total enrollment of 2,000 are taking college-preparatory courses.

"Further, he will say, 1,070 students this year are taking mathematics—including beginning and advanced algebra, plane and solid geometry and trigonometry—and 1,046 are taking science, including physics, chemistry, physiology, and biology."

One of the canons of journalism is that conflict makes news. So our mass media in the past few years have featured denunciations, viewings with alarm, jeremiads and the voices of assorted Cassandras newly become expert on elementary and secondary education. The air waves and the printed pages have been clogged with revelations on the deficiencies of public education by developers of atomic submarines, historians prospecting in the educational wastelands, and college presidents enjoying a respite from liberal arts campus problems of student misdemeanors. Anger is newsworthy; for instance a journalist might judge the above sentence the only one worthy of quotation in this entire context. The infection has spread even to the book industry which is vital to free communication of ideas; an editor for the general public casually commented recently, "Only angry books on education ever sell."

In the sound and fury which accompanied the Great Panic, a crucial issue for American life has been obscured. That issue is: should American education train manpower or educate individuals? Scratch a sponsor of the Great Panic, and even some of the bandwagon-riding unscholarly scholars, and you find one who views people as manpower, pawns to be manipulated, faceless men to be assigned. Preferable is the view of novelist John Hersey who stated the issue eloquently in *Intelligence, Choice and Consent*:

"The failure here is a failure of national vision—for we have tended to see human beings as statistics, children as weapons, talents as materials capable of being mined, assayed, and fabricated for profit and defense. We have the cart before the horse if we think that we can order up units of talent for the national defense. The only sure defense of democracy will be its inner growth, and the first essential of this growth is something far less grandiose but far more difficult of realization than a National Defense Education Act, or a crash program under any other title—namely, a true recognition that each child in each classroom in our schools is a unique human being, who one day must make choices and give consents that will help to perfect us all."

In the era of the Great Panic, not enough professional educators have stood up to be counted. Too few have declared themselves for the development of social understanding, for a varied special education, for a balanced curriculum, for the education of individual persons. Professional educators should have said to the people, "I am not ready to accept the communist education of the Soviet Union as a model for the United States. I am not ready to accept for the children and youth of my country a program of Death Adjustment Education."

Too many in professional leadership positions have abdicated responsibility for rigorous participation in the Great Debate. Refuge has been taken in the slogan, "The schools belong to the people." Of course the schools belong to the people but a corollary sometimes has been forgotten: "The obligation of the schoolman is to exert leadership." At a time when many professional educators have adopted the barometer theory of education, simply registering and responding to the pressures from the surrounding atmosphere, the fable of the animals and their school system may be apropos:

"Once upon a time, there lived in the deep forest a father squirrel who was dissatisfied with the forest school system. Though his son went to school and the teacher tried hard to educate him, his son still persisted in acting like a squirrel. So father squirrel dropped an acorn on the superintendent's roof. The rabbit who served as superintendent of the forest system heard the acorn crash. He immediately concluded that the entire lay public of the forest was bombarding the school. So he lit out for the nearest rabbit hole. There wasn't room in the hole for both the rabbit and his principles (to say nothing of his curriculum director). So he carefully placed his principles under a leaf before he scuttled down the hole. He figured the principles might come in handy sometime if he needed a philosophy of education or had to make a speech. He was a rabbit, so naturally he didn't feel sheepish about this . . ."

Substitute all of us in the profession for the rabbit superintendent, exempt the many honorable exceptions who have fought for their principles of democratic education, and the fable comes too close to home to be comfortable.

Into the vacuum created by the abdication of professional leadership came James B. Conant. A quiet and effective man, unrivalled in prestige, he presented in 1959 in *The American High School Today* many valid recommendations. My own point of view on the Conant Report might best be described by excerpts from my review in *Education Leadership*, October, 1959.

"There is much in James B. Conant's first report with which we are in agreement. Section One, "The Characteristics of American Education," is an eloquent case for the comprehensive American high school. With reason and historical evidence it cuts ground from under the selective academic schools and the class-perpetuating European system so dear to the nostalgia of Admiral Rickover. The Conant Report calls on the comprehensive American high school, "first, to provide a good general education for all the future citizens; second, to provide good elective programs for those who wish to use their acquired skills immediately on graduation; third, to provide satisfactory programs for those whose vocations will depend on their subsequent education in college or university." Thus the Report rejects the Robert Hutchins philosophy which prizes the academic for all who manage to stay in school and which heaps anathema upon vocational learnings.

"James B. Conant states as his top priority the elimination of the small high school, thus joining the legion of modern educators who have fought stoutly for consolidation. In an era of the flight to centralized authority, he quietly asserts 'that three things are necessary to have a good high school, provided it is of sufficient size: first, a school board composed of devoted, intelligent, understanding citizens who realize fully the distinction between policy making and administration; second, a first-rate superintendent; and third, a good principal.' (We suspect he wouldn't mind if we added the forgotten fourth and fifth, "good supervisors" and "good teachers.")

"In addition, the Report supports an expanded counseling system (Rec. 1), individualized programs (Rec. 2), required programs for all (Rec. 3), expansion of writing (Rec. 6), diversified education programs (Rec. 7), remedial reading (Rec. 8), provision for talented and gifted (Rec. 9, 10), prerequisites for advanced courses (Rec. 13), avoidance of ranking (Rec. 14), developmental reading (Rec. 16), tuition-free summer schools (Rec. 17), offering a third and fourth year of languages (Rec. 18), science courses (Rec. 19), homerooms (Rec. 20), a problems-oriented 12th grade social studies (Rec. 21). Surely, all of these sound reasonable.

"With what in the Conant Report, then, do we fundamentally disagree?

"First of all, the Report conceives the vital matters of curriculum as quantitative. For instance, for the academically talented 15 to 20 per cent, the Report strongly recommends as a minimum 'four years of mathematics, four years of one foreign language, three years of science, in addition to the required four years of English and three years of social studies; a total of eighteen courses with homework to be taken in four years. This program will require at least fifteen hours of homework each week.' The Report continues, 'Many academically talented pupils may wish to study a second foreign language or an additional course in social studies. Since such students are capable of handling twenty or more courses, these additional academic courses may be added to the recommended minimum program.'

"The Report assumes, without questioning, that proliferation of many subjects is better than concentration upon fewer, that four of something is necessarily better than two or three, that twenty or more courses during the high school years are better than sixteen, that a seven or eight period day is better than one with a block of time for a core, that fifteen hours of homework of undefined quality ("hard work") is necessarily better than any other family or community learnings.

"Almost completely neglected is the crux of the curriculum problem: what goes on within the courses. Untouched is the vital matter of the meaningfulness of the learning experiences to the young person. Unexamined is the quality of the learning. Thus the report repeatedly deals with the shadow, not the substance, of the curriculum.

"What seems to have happened is that a gifted and good man has visited some American high schools, including 'in many cases, a visit to one or more classes,' and has recommended, particularly for the academically talented, a program which reflects his own cultural background and life experiences. Dr. Conant is an eminent scientist who knows the complexities of higher mathematics. To him it is self-evident that the policy to be adopted to serve as 'a guide' to the counselors of the talented should include four years of mathematics and three years of science. So self-evident is this that nowhere in the Report is the all-but-required extensive mathematics and science program for the talented specifically supported, save by one reference to vocational uses of the sciences. Yet other gifted and good men regard four years of social studies (not recommended as a minimum by the Report) and four years of the varied arts (not recommended as a minimum by the Report) as at least as defensible as a minimum for the talented, if the standard is to be quantitative.

"James B. Conant and his staff have prepared an earnest and provocative contribution to the Great Debate. A scholar of Dr. Conant's quality knows that his inquiry has human and scholarly limitations as well as deep insights. Let us hope that the razzle dazzle of publicity which has surrounded the Report will not result in the Twenty One Recommendations (however useful many will prove) being mistaken for the Ten Commandments."

Nevertheless the Twenty One Recommendations have sometimes been taken for the Ten Commandments and some have confused Dr. Conant's offices with Mount Sinai. In some school systems professional personnel have been called to account by board members because recommendation X or Y was not in operation, thus keeping the system from having "a Conant high school." We have even heard of a schoolman who reported to his patrons that his school had gone beyond being a Conant high school and had become an Admiral Rickover high school!

The relative lack of close examination of the Conant recommendations reflects a quest for certainty by the public and the profession. Certainty is promoted by a quantitative approach, emphasis on organizational structure, concrete recommendations. Yet a few of us stubbornly suspect that despite the hunger for certainty we must live by qualitative principles such as these, rather than by quantitative units:

We believe that secondary education should include both general education and the richest possible program of specialized education.

We believe that secondary education in this American democracy should be dedicated to helping each and every boy and girl develop into the best that he is capable of becoming.

We believe that secondary schools should be a major unifying force for the development of the democratic idea among young people of varied races, religions, nationalities, and social classes.

We believe in the fundamental importance of knowledge and the surpassing importance of the basic question, "knowledge for what?"

We believe that high school youngsters are individuals, characterized by individual differences and a variety of needs and interests.

We believe that a range of experiences within the curriculum and a variety of methods and materials and groupings will best serve high school students.

We believe that motivation and the stimulation of intellectual curiosity through adults who understand youth are essential to valuable learning experiences.

We believe that thinking is best fostered by the solving of problems which are real and important to high school young people.

We believe that education is a process, not simply of pouring in, but of steadily cultivating meaningful learning experiences and reflective judgment.

We believe that the high school must come to grips with the needs, problems, and tensions of the learner.

We believe that the high school must help young people become aware of the social realities of our times and help them relate themselves to the social demands of the surrounding culture.

We believe that the high school must teach young people to understand and practice the democratic way of life characterized by respect for individual personality, common concern for human welfare, and the development of reflective thinking.

The nineteen sixties bring a second Conant report focussing on the junior high school years. The coming recommendations were foreshadowed by Dr. Conant before the American Association of School Administrators in Atlantic City in February and before the National Association of Secondary School Principals in Portland in early March.

The *New York Times* of February 16, 1960 reported of Conant's Atlantic City speech:

"Dr. Conant suggested tentatively that the eighth grade be 'fully departmentalized,' with specialized teachers in every subject, and that the seventh grade be considered 'a transition' between the self-contained class, with one teacher in charge of most subjects, and the departmentalization of high school."

The *New York Herald Tribune* of the same date reported:

"Dr. Conant said that he was 'convinced' that the eighth grade should be departmentalized into eight subjects: English, social studies, mathematics, science, art, music, home economics and the industrial arts. 'I believe,' he said, 'that all these eight subjects should be required of all pupils in Grade 8 or in Grades 7 and 8, though the last four need not be studied every day.' Specialized teachers should teach these eight courses, he added. He also advocated a period of physical education for all pupils in Grades 1 through 12 every day."

On March 3, 1960, the *New York Times* began its report on Dr. Conant's Portland speech as follows:

"The junior high school must help to re-establish the balance between the 'child-centered' elementary school and the 'subject-centered' high school and college, Dr. James B. Conant told the annual convention of National Association of Secondary School Principals here today.

"Dr. Conant reminded the educators that the junior high schools were originally intended to teach such subjects as algebra and foreign languages, but that these purposes were lost in the Nineteen Twenties. The child-centered viewpoint gained the upper hand, Dr. Conant said, and 'concern with subject matter retreated towards the senior high schools.' "

Professional educators should say to Dr. Conant with respect, courtesy, and firmness, "Sir, we do not support a child-centered elementary school. Nor do we support a subject-centered high school and college. Instead, we support at all levels—elementary, junior high, senior high, and college—an education that deals with social realities and appropriate social demands, that meets the needs of learners, and that develops democratic values. We are well aware that both individual development and realistically conceived national needs are important.

"On the junior high school level we cannot reconcile strict departmentalization with your worthy goals of sufficient guidance, expanded writing, and avoidance of undue academic pressures. We believe the junior high school should include a daily block of time, two or three class periods in length, primarily centered on social understanding through study of personal-social problems. Such a core of the curriculum gives one teacher time to really know individual students and to foster and work with abundant writing, while avoiding excessive pressures on youngsters. In addition to the daily block of time absorbing at least social studies and English, junior high school youth should have opportunities for study in varied courses in science, mathematics, and world languages, some required and some freely chosen; for experiences in the several arts, physical education, and student activities, also some required and some freely chosen. Each course, each experience, should be geared to the widely differing talents and needs of early adolescents."

The professional educators must rejoin the Great Debate. Not defensively, not in defense of the status quo, not as spokesman for complacency. We too belong to the worried though we refuse to join the panic-stricken. We probably know better than our friendly advisers and our extremist critics what is really wrong with our schools!

Educational leadership has a two-fold task. We must push forward the frontiers of knowledge through research and experimentation. But we must also speak out loudly and clearly as best we can for the best we now know. We now know that education for social understanding is crucial. We now know that a varied program of special education leading youth into many fields is demanded by the future. We now know that balance in the curriculum is needed. We now know that we are not training manpower but educating unique human beings to make choices.